BioCritiques

Bloom's BioCritiques

STEPHEN KING

Edited and with an introduction by
Harold Bloom
Sterling Professor of the Humanities
Yale University

CHELSEA HOUSE PUBLISHERS
Philadelphia

©2002 by Chelsea House Publishers, a subsidiary of
Haights Cross Communications.

Introduction © 2002 by Harold Bloom.

Printed and bound in the United States of America

10 9 8 7 6 5 4 3 2 1

Library of Congress Cataloging-in-Publication Data

Stephen King / Harold Bloom, ed.
        p. cm — (Bloom's Biocritiques)
Includes bibliographical references and index.
   ISBN 0-7910-6178-7 – 0-7910-7173-1 (pbk.)
   1. King, Stephen, 1947- 2. Novelists, American—20th
century—Biography. 3. Horror tales, American—History and criticism.
I. Bloom, Harold. II. Series.
   PS3561.I483 Z878 2002
   813'.54—dc21

                                                2002005481

Chelsea House Publishers
1974 Sproul Road, Suite 400
Broomall, PA 19008-0914

http://www.chelseahouse.com

Contributing editor: Aimee LaBrie

Layout by EJB Publishing Services

24.95

CONTENTS

491420

User's Guide

These volumes are designed to introduce the reader to the life and work of the world's literary masters. Each volume begins with Harold Bloom's essay "The Work in the Writer" and a volume-specific introduction also written by Professor Bloom. Following these unique introductions is an engaging biography that discusses the major life events and important literary accomplishments of the author under consideration.

Furthermore, each volume includes an original critique that not only traces the themes, symbols, and ideas apparent in the author's works, but strives to put those works into cultural and historical perspectives. In addition to the original critique is a brief selection of significant critical essays previously published on the author and his or her works followed by a concise and informative chronology of the writer's life. Finally, each volume concludes with a bibliography of the writer's works, a list of additional readings, and an index of important themes and ideas.

HAROLD BLOOM

The Work in the Writer

Literary biography found its masterpiece in James Boswell's *Life of Samuel Johnson*. Boswell, when he treated Johnson's writings, implicitly commented upon Johnson as found in his work, even as in the great critic's life. Modern instances of literary biography, such as Richard Ellmann's lives of W. B. Yeats, James Joyce, and Oscar Wilde, essentially follow in Boswell's pattern.

That the writer somehow is in the work, we need not doubt, though with William Shakespeare, writer-of-writers, we almost always need to rely upon pure surmise. The exquisite rancidities of the Problem Plays or Dark Comedies seem to express an extraordinary estrangement of Shakespeare from himself. When we read or attend *Troilus and Cressida* and *Measure for Measure*, we may be startled by particular speeches of Ulysses in the first play, or of Vincentio in the second. These speeches, of Ulysses upon hierarchy or upon time, or of Duke Vincentio upon death, are too strong either for their contexts or for the characters of their speakers. The same phenomenon occurs with Parolles, the military impostor of *All's Well That Ends Well*. Utterly disgraced, he nevertheless affirms: "Simply the thing I am/Shall make me live."

In Shakespeare, more even than in his peers, Dante and Cervantes, meaning always starts itself again through excess or overflow. The strongest of Shakespeare's creatures—Falstaff, Hamlet, Iago, Lear, Cleopatra—have an exuberance that is fiercer than their plays can contain. If Ben Jonson was at all correct in his complaint that "Shakespeare wanted art," it could have been only in a sense that he may not have intended. Where do the personalities of Falstaff or Hamlet touch a limit? What was it in Shakespeare that made the two parts of *Henry IV* and *Hamlet* into "plays unlimited"? Neither Falstaff nor Hamlet will be stopped: their wit, their beautiful, laughing speech, their intensity of being—all these are virtually infinite.

In what ways do Falstaff and Hamlet manifest the writer in the work? Evidently, we can never know, or know enough to answer with any authority. But what would happen if we reversed the question, and asked: How did the work form the writer, Shakespeare?

Of Shakespeare's inwardness, his biography tells us nothing. And yet, to an astonishing extent, Shakespeare created our inwardness. At the least, we can speculate that Shakespeare so lived his life as to conceal the depths of his nature, particularly as he rather prematurely aged. We do not have Shakespeare on Shakespeare, as any good reader of the Sonnets comes to realize: they do not constitute a key that unlocks his heart. No sequence of sonnets could be less confessional or more powerfully detached from the poet's self.

The German poet and universal genius, Goethe, affords a superb contrast to Shakespeare. Of Goethe's life, we know more than everything; I wonder sometimes if we know as much about Napoleon or Freud or any other human being who ever has lived, as we know about Goethe. Everywhere, we can find Goethe in his work, so much so that Goethe seems to crowd the writing out, just as Byron and Oscar Wilde seem to usurp their own literary accomplishments. Goethe, cunning beyond measure, nevertheless invested a rival exuberance in his greatest works that could match his personal charisma. The sublime outrageousness of the Second Part of *Faust*, or of the greater lyric and meditative poems, form a Counter-Sublime to Goethe's own daemonic intensity.

Goethe was fascinated by the daemonic in himself; we can doubt that Shakespeare had any such interests. Evidently, Shakespeare abandoned his acting career just before he composed *Measure for Measure* and *Othello*. I surmise that the egregious interventions by Vincentio and Iago displace the actor's energies into a new kind of mischief-making, a fresh opening to a subtler playwriting-within-the-play.

But what had opened Shakespeare to this new awareness? The answer is the work in the writer, *Hamlet* in Shakespeare. One can go further: it was not so much the play, *Hamlet*, as the character Hamlet, who changed Shakespeare's art forever.

Hamlet's personality is so large and varied that it rivals Goethe's own. Ironically Goethe's Faust, his Hamlet, has no personality at all, and is as colorless as Shakespeare himself seems to have chosen to be. Yet nothing could be more colorful than the Second Part of *Faust*, which is peopled by an astonishing array of monsters, grotesque devils, and classical ghosts.

A contrast between Shakespeare and Goethe demonstrates that in each—but in very different ways—we can better find the work in the person, than we can discover that banal entity, the person in the work. Goethe to many of his contemporaries, seemed to be a mortal god. Shakespeare, so far as we know, seemed an affable, rather ordinary fellow, who aged early and became somewhat withdrawn. Yet Faust, though Mephistopheles battles for his soul, is hardly worth the trouble unless you take him as an idea and not as a person. Hamlet is nearly every-idea-in-one, but he is precisely a personality and a person.

Would Hamlet be so astonishingly persuasive if his father's ghost did not haunt him? Falstaff is more alive than Prince Hal, who says that the devil haunts him in the shape of an old fat man. Three years before composing the final *Hamlet*, Shakespeare invented Falstaff, who then never ceased to haunt his creator. Falstaff and Hamlet may be said to best represent the work in the writer, because their influence upon Shakespeare was prodigious. W.H. Auden accurately observed that Falstaff possesses infinite energy: never tired, never bored, and absolutely both witty and happy until Hal's rejection destroys him. Hamlet too has infinite energy, but in him it is more curse than blessing.

Falstaff and Hamlet can be said to occupy the roles in Shakespeare's invented world that Sancho Panza and Don Quixote possess in Cervantes's. Shakespeare's plays from 1610 on (starting with *Twelfth Night*) are thus analogous to the Second Part of Cervantes's epic novel. Sancho and the Don overtly jostle Cervantes for authorship in the Second Part, even as Cervantes battles against the impostor who has pirated a continuation of his work. As a dramatist, Shakespeare manifests the work in the writer more indirectly. Falstaff's prose genius is revived in the scapegoating of Malvolio by Maria and Sir Toby Belch, while Falstaff's darker insights are developed by Feste's melancholic wit. Hamlet's intellectual resourcefulness, already deadly, becomes poisonous in Iago and in Edmund. Yet we have not crossed into the deeper abysses of the work in the writer in later Shakespeare.

No fictive character, before or since, is Falstaff's equal in self-trust. Sir John, whose delight in himself is contagious, has total confidence both in his self-awareness and in the resources of his language. Hamlet, whose self is as strong, and whose language is as copious, nevertheless distrusts both the self and language. Later Shakespeare is, as it were, much under the influence both of Falstaff and of Hamlet, but they tug him in opposite directions. Shakespeare's own copiousness of language is well-nigh incredible: a vocabulary in excess of twenty-one thousand words, almost eighteen hundred of which he coined himself. And of his word-hoard, nearly half are used only once each, as though the perfect setting for each had been found, and need not be repeated. Love for language and faith in language are Falstaffian attributes. Hamlet will darken both that love and that faith in Shakespeare, and perhaps the Sonnets can best be read as Falstaff and Hamlet counterpointing against one another.

Can we surmise how aware Shakespeare was of Falstaff and Hamlet, once they had played themselves into existence? *Henry IV, Part I* appeared in six quarto editions during Shakespeare's lifetime; *Hamlet* possibly had four. Falstaff and Hamlet were played again and again at the Globe, but Shakespeare knew also that they were being read, and he must have had contact with some of those readers. What would it have been like to discuss Falstaff or Hamlet with one of their early readers (presumably also part of their audience at the Globe), if you were the creator of such demiurges? The question would seem nonsensical to most Shakespeare scholars, but then these days they tend to be either ideologues or moldy figs. How can we recover the uncanniness of Falstaff and of Hamlet, when they now have become so familiar?

A writer's influence upon himself is an unexplored problem in criticism, but such an influence is never free from anxieties. The biocritical problem (which this series attempts to explore) can be divided into two areas, difficult to disengage fully. Accomplished works affect the author's life, and also affect her subsequent writings. It is simpler for me to surmise the effect of *Mrs. Dalloway* and *To the Lighthouse* upon Woolf's late *Between the Acts*, than it is to relate Clarissa Dalloway's suicide and Lily Briscoe's capable endurance in art to the tragic death and complex life of Virginia Woolf.

There are writers whose lives were so vivid that they seem sometimes to obscure the literary achievement: Byron, Wilde, Malraux, Hemingway. But most major Western writers do not live that exuberantly, and the greatest of all, Shakespeare, sometimes appears to have adopted the personal mask of colorlessness. And yet there are heroes of literature who struggled titanically with their own eras—Tolstoy, Milton, Victor Hugo—who nevertheless matter more for their works than their lives.

There are great figures—Emily Dickinson, Wallace Stevens, Willa Cather—who seem to have had so little of the full intensity of life when compared to the vitality of their work, that we might almost speak of the work in the work, rather than even of the work in a person. Emily Brontë might well be the extreme instance of such a visionary, surpassing William Blake in that one regard.

I conclude this general introduction to a series of literary bio-critiques by stating a tentative formula or principle for gauging the many ways in which the work influences the person and her subsequent, later work. Our influence upon ourselves is always related to the Shakespearean invention of self-overhearing, which I have written about in several other contexts. Life, as well as poetry and prose, is overheard rather than simply heard. The writer listens to herself as though she were somebody else, and the will to change begins to operate. The forces that live in us include the prior work we have done, and the dreams and waking visions that evade our dismissals.

HAROLD BLOOM

Introduction

By all accounts, Stephen King is public-spirited, generous, humane, and an exemplary social citizen. As a novelist and story-writer, he impresses me as being no more or less aesthetically and cognitively valuable than Tom Clancy, Danielle Steele, John Grisham, and our other popular novelists with enormous audiences. That is to say, King—like these others—does not seem to me a borderline literary phenomenon, whose works will have the status of period pieces. Rather, King's books—like Clancy's and Grisham's—are not literary at all, in my critical judgment. I am aware that there is much opinion opposing me upon this matter. Recently, the editor of a mass-circulation magazine asked me to write an aesthetic defense of King, who in the editor's judgment is the Charles Dickens of our time. Schoolchildren, encouraged to read over the summer, make their way through one or two volumes of King. Reading *Harry Potter* is not reading, and neither is perusing Stephen King. He, more than the sci-fi authors, is the writer who is consonant with our age of virtual reality. The screen, the World Wide Web, and Stephen King are different aspects of the one eclipse of reading.

King, whatever his qualities, emerges from an American tradition one could regard as sub-literary: Poe and H. P. Lovecraft. Lovecraft revered Poe, though he also followed the British fantasist Arthur Machen. In King's instance, the direct precursor would seem to be Jack London, later to be replaced by Lovecraft and Poe and then by an entire range of popular horror fiction.

Alexander Pope warned against breaking a butterfly upon a wheel, so I will avoid King's obvious inadequacies: cliché-writing, flat characters who are names upon the page, and in general a remarkable absence of invention for someone edging over into the occult, the preternatural, the imaginary. Nothing is justifiable about Poe's prose (or his verse), but Poe dreamed or constructed universal and permanent nightmares. Lovecraft, whom I find very hard to get through, nevertheless receives a cogent defense in a great book of exegesis, Victoria Nelson's *The Secret Life of Puppets* (2001). For Nelson, Lovecraft takes us back to the major ancient and Renaissance heresies: Neoplatonism, Hermeticism, Gnosticism.

Part of Lovecraft's peculiar power may be this deep link to ancient heresies, but I hardly believe that King would be improved as a writer by an immersion in Neoplatonism. An esoteric cosmogony would be of little use to King, who is a horror-writer rather than a creator of romance-fantasies. His fans find exactly what they want in King, and these are fans he shares with Anne Rice (a sickly imagination) and with Dean Koontz and Peter Straub, who are less homespun than King.

I persist in my impression that King's books are not *written*, as such. They are visually oriented scenarios, and they tend to improve when filmed. And there is the largest clue I can discover for his enormous circulation: he is the crucial horror-writer called forth by the Age of Information. He persuades his legions of fans because his monstrosities are presented *as information*.

CINDY DYSON

Biography of Stephen King

FURNACE ROOM MUSINGS

With his long legs buckled under a child's desk, Stephen King hunched over his typewriter in the trailer's tiny furnace room. Through the thin walls, he occasionally heard the shouts and jabbering of his two small children over the clicking keys. He began his story with a lonely teenage girl in the shower room at school, humiliated and ostracized by her classmates. He mused: What if the girl that nobody likes wanted revenge and had the power to kill with her mind?

After a few pages, he tossed it into the trash. What did he know about high school girls? He'd been writing for years now, selling a few stories in men's magazines. But the last novel he'd tried to sell, a science fiction tale, had only brought another round of rejections. King unfolded himself from his desk and shut the furnace room door on the first few pages of his latest failure.

The next evening, when King came home from work, his wife, Tabitha ("Tabby"), had the pages in hand. She'd taken the crumpled, ash-smeared pages from the garbage. "She wanted to know the rest of the story," King remembered. "I told her I didn't know jack shit about high school girls. She said she'd help me with that part. She had her chin tilted down and was smiling in that severely cute way of hers. 'You've got something here,' she said. 'I really think you do.'"

Invigorated, he continued writing, and several months later he sent the manuscript of *Carrie* off to Doubleday, a publishing house that had rejected

3

his previous works but whose editor, Bill Thompson, had been encouraging. A few weeks passed before King got "the call." Thompson asked him to go to New York City for an informal lunch with some important persons from Doubleday. Borrowing $75 from Tabitha's grandmother, King bought some new shoes and caught a bus to New York.

He arrived in New York at 6 a.m., before the sun came up, and had to pass the time until the appointment. He walked around anxiously, thinking of possibilities. As King recalls:

> I had blisters on both feet because I had foolishly worn a new pair of shoes purchased especially for the trip. My neck hurt from doing the famous out-of-town, country-boy, my-look-at-them-tall-buildings crane. I had not slept on the bus the night before, ordered two gin-and-tonics and was almost immediately struck drunk. I had never been so determined to make no glaring social gaffe and never so convinced (at least since the night of my high school junior prom) that I would make one. To top it off, I ordered fettuccini, a dish bearded young men should avoid.

Despite the fettuccini, King left the meeting thinking he had a chance. One March afternoon in 1973, as King was in the teacher's room, grading papers, the intercom summoned him to the office. He had a call from his wife.

"I hurried, not quite running, my heart beating hard," King said. "Tabby would have had to dress the kids in their boots and jackets to use the neighbors' phone, and I could think of only two reasons she might have done so. Either Joe or Naomi had fallen off the stoop and broken a leg, or I had sold *Carrie*."

Thompson had sent a telegram—the Kings had disconnected the phone to cut expenses—Doubleday was offering him a $2,500 advance for hardcover rights.

"After about 1,500 pages of unpublished manuscripts," King said, "I was a bona fide first novelist."

On Mother's Day, Thompson called with even better news. New American Library had just bought the paperback rights to *Carrie*. While it was common for one publishing house to bring out a book in hardback, and then sell the paperback rights to another house, the $400,000 offer was uncommon for a first novel. "I called him back that night, at his home, convinced that what he had actually said was $40,000," King remembered. "And for the next two or three weeks, I lived with a constant, nagging fear that somebody would call and tell me it had all been a mistake or a misunderstanding."

Tabitha and the kids weren't home yet. King rushed out to find a present for Tabitha—a thank-you for believing in him, a harbinger of the good life ahead. All he could find was a $16.95 hair dryer. When she got home, he handed it to her.

"She looked at it as if she'd never seen one before," King remembered. "'What's this for?' she asked. I took her by the shoulders. I told her about the paperback sale. She didn't appear to understand. I told her again. Tabby looked over my shoulder at our shitty little four-room apartment, just as I had, and began to cry."

Stephen King has been a publishing superstar for decades now, and he is perhaps the most published, prolific, and well-paid author of his generation. His work has changed the horror genre and blurred the lines between horror and literary fiction.

THE EARLY YEARS

Donald and Ruth King were living in Portland, Maine, on September 21, 1947, when their second child, Stephen Edwin King, was born. Stephen was a surprise to the young couple who had been told they wouldn't be able to have children of their own; two years prior to Stephen's birth, they had adopted David King as an infant.

Donald was a vacuum salesman who had served in the merchant marine. He was a handsome, well-liked man, but a man King would never know. In 1949, when King was only two years old, Donald walked out of the house and never came back. "Actually, it was a classic desertion," King has said, "not even a note of explanation or justification left behind. He said, literally, that he was going out to the grocery store for a pack of cigarettes, and he didn't take any of his things with him. That was in 1949, and none of us have heard of the bastard since." With two small boys and little money, King's mother shuffled the family around the country for the next few years, staying with relatives in Maine, Massachusetts, Illinois, Wisconsin, Texas, and Connecticut.

King's fear of and fascination with the macabre began when he was only a toddler. He remembers:

> According to Mom, I had gone off to play at a neighbor's house—a house that was near a railroad line. About an hour after I left I came back (she said), as white as a ghost. I would not speak for the rest of that day; I would not tell her . . . why my chum's mom hadn't walked me back, but allowed me to come home alone. It turned out that the kid I had been playing with had been

run over by a freight train while playing or crossing the tracks. Years later, my mother told me they had picked up the pieces in a wicker basket . . .

Although King does not remember what he saw, trains would become a deadly force in many of his books.

Ruth worked many menial jobs to support her two sons. She held jobs as a laundry presser, a doughnut maker, a store clerk, a housekeeper, and a pianist. In addition to financially supporting her family, Ruth King also passed on her love of books, calling the stacks of paperbacks often lying about "a pile of cheap, sweet vacations."

King spent much of his sixth year in bed, sick with tonsillitis and ear infections. To pass the time, he read comic books and copied the stories onto paper. When he showed one to his mother, she asked him whether he had made up the stories himself. He admitted he had not. "Write one of your own, Stevie," she said. "Those *Combat Casey* funny-books are just junk . . . I bet you could do better. Write one of your own."

"I remember an immense feeling of *possibility* at the idea," King recalled, "as if I had been ushered into a vast building filled with closed doors and had been given leave to open any I liked." Soon he had finished a four-page penciled story about a bunny that could drive a car. He gave it to his mother, who told him it was good enough to be a book. "Nothing anyone has said to me since," King said, "has made me feel any happier."

When he was seven, Ruth introduced King to the world of horror novels:

> She had a thin book from the library—obviously a grown-up book. You always knew the difference, because they were dull on the outside, but sometimes interesting on the inside. I said, "What's that one about?" And she said, "Oh, you wouldn't like this one. This one's a really scary one. It's about a man who changes into someone else. It's called *The Strange Case of Dr. Jekyll and Mr. Hyde*." And I said, "Read it to me." And she protested, but never very hard, because she loved that stuff. . . . I lived and died with that story . . . with Dr. Jekyll's other side, which was every vestige of pretense of civilization thrown away. I can remember lying in bed, wakeful after that night's reading was done.

At seven, King also saw his first horror movie: he went to the drive-in with his mother and her date to see *The Creature from the Black Lagoon*. It influenced his ability to incorporate description into his writing. "I still see things cinematically," King has said years later. "I write down everything I see. It seems like a movie to me, and I write that way." And it was in this way that he wrote his first horror story, at about the same age: A dinosaur terrorizes a town. No one can vanquish the beast until a clever scientist discovers the dinosaur's allergy to leather. The townspeople assault the dinosaur with leather objects until it flees.

When King was 11, in 1958, Ruth King moved her boys to the small, working-class town of Durham, Maine, where she could take care of her ageing parents. The Kings rented a two-story house with an outhouse and a well that frequently went dry. King and David hauled buckets of water from a nearby spring every summer, and relatives brought food and second-hand clothing to Ruth and the boys.

"I guess in many ways it was a hard-scrabble existence but not an impoverished one in the most important sense of the word," King recalls. "Thanks to my mother, the one thing that was never in short supply, corny as it may sound to say it, was love. And in that sense, I was a hell of a lot less deprived than countless children of middle-class or wealthy families, whose parents have time for everything but their kids."

Despite his mother's love, King still longed for his father. Then one day, as he and David were exploring their aunt's attic, they found a collection of items that had belonged to their father. In a forgotten box were piles of their father's paperbacks, unpublished stories Donald had written, and a home movie of his years in the merchant marines. Eager to see it, the two rented a movie projector:

> When we finally got it working, the stuff was pretty disappointing at first—a lot of strange faces and exotic scenes but no sign of the old man. And then, after we'd gone through a couple of reels of film, David jumped up and said, "That's him! That's our father!" He'd handed the camera to one of his buddies and there he was, lounging against a ship's rail, a choppy sea in the background. My old man. David remembered him, but it was a stranger's face to me. . . . He raised his hand and smiled, unwittingly waving at sons who weren't born yet. "Hi, Dad, don't forget to write."

Here was the man who hadn't cared enough to stay. The emotional blow was part of King's early attraction to horror stories, where could lose himself in other worlds—worlds in which heroes lived and fought evil with the hard eyes and courage of the father he should have had. "Without a father," King has explained, "I needed my own power trips."

Growing up, King was a big, klutzy kid, his eyes always glued to a book. His black hair stuck out at odd angles; his glasses were thick, and his front teeth protruded. He was the guy who was picked last for sports teams. On the outside he was awkward, hesitant; on the inside he was angry that his father had left. This shy, wounded boy would turn up again and again in his books as a sort of hero in disguise.

With their mother working long hours, the King brothers were often left to their own devices. The two "latchkey kids" transformed an old shed behind their house into a clubhouse and spent summer vacations hanging out with friends, playing cards, and reading magazines. The boys ran through a nearby cemetery, listened to Elvis Presley, read Ray Bradbury. They earned good grades and went to every movie that they could.

King and his friend Chris Chesley even got a home movie camera and experimented with techniques for building suspense on film. In fact, it was while watching a film that King felt the biggest scare of his young life—one that taught him about the connection between the fears we imagine and the real ones lurking in everyday life. He was watching *Earth vs. the Flying Saucers* in 1957 when, in the middle of the movie, the house lights came on and the theater manager strode to the front. He announced that Russia had just launched a satellite, called Sputnik, into orbit. King recalls:

> There was a long, hushed pause as this crowd of '50s kids in cuffed jeans, with crewcuts or ducktails or ponytails, struggled to absorb all that. And then, suddenly, one voice, near tears but also charged with terrible anger, shrilled through the stunned silence: "Oh, go show the movie, you liar!" And after a few minutes, the film came back on, but I just sat there, frozen to my seat, because I knew the manager wasn't lying. . . . I immediately made the connection between the film we were seeing and the fact that the Russians had a space satellite circling the heavens, loaded, for all I knew, with H-bombs to rain down on our unsuspecting heads. And at that moment, the fears of fictional horror vividly intersected with the reality of potential nuclear holocaust; a transition from fantasy to a real world suddenly became far more ominous and threatening. And as I sat there, the film concluded with the voices of the malignant invading saucerians echoing from the screen in a final threat: "Look to your skies. . . . A warning will come from your skies. . . . Look to your skies. . . ." I still find it impossible to convey, even to my own kids, how terribly frightened and alone and depressed I felt at that moment.

IMAGINATION UNLEASHED

In spite of his strange looks and his awkwardness, King achieved his own kind of popularity at school: he was the kid who could write. In elementary school, he wrote a story about his classmates being held hostage. He used real names and quickly killed off students he didn't like, letting the ones he did like live longer and even become the heroes. Eventually all in the story die fighting the National Guard, but King had written himself into a bit of popularity. Now kids wanted to be his friend—to have a shot a playing the hero next time.

Friends would come to the King house to listen to the stories he pounded out on a manual typewriter in the bedroom he shared with David. His friend Chris recalls:

> When I went to Stephen King's house to write stories with him, there was the sense that these things weren't just stories; when you walked inside the walls of his house, there was a sense of palpability, almost as if the characters in the stories had real weight. . . . It was a world unto itself, and I was privileged to enter it. Even as a kid, as a teenager, King had the power to do that.

In January of 1959, David began publishing his own newspaper, called *Dave's Rag*, on which King was a reporter, covering television and town events. Eventually the paper had 20 paid subscriptions. In the paper's classifieds, King began trying to sell his stories. "New book by STEVE KING!" one advertisement announced. Another offered, "Land of 1,000,000 Years Ago. Exciting story of 21 people (who were) prisoners on an island that should have been extinct 1,000,000 years ago. Order through this newspaper."

Seeking a larger market, King tried to sell his stories at school, too. In 1961, after seeing Roger Corman's *The Pit and the Pendulum*, King wrote his own version. He made 40 copies of the eight-page book, selling them for a quarter each. He remembered:

> I took the entire print run to school in my book-bag . . . and by noon that day I had sold two dozen. By the end lunch hour, when word had gotten around about the lady buried in the wall . . . I had sold three dozen. I had nine dollars in change weighing down the bottom of my book-bag . . . and was walking around in a kind of dream, unable to believe my sudden ascension to

previously unsuspected realms of wealth. It all seemed too good to be true.

It was. The school's principal summoned him and insisted that the school was not a marketplace. However, it was a teacher whose comments disturbed King the most:

> "What I don't understand, Stevie," she said, "is why you'd write junk like this in the first place. You're talented. Why do you want to waste your abilities?" She had rolled up a copy of (the book) and was brandishing it at me the way a person might brandish a rolled-up newspaper at a dog that has piddled on the rug. . . . I was ashamed. I have spent a good may years since—too many, I think—being ashamed about what I write.

While King had to give back all the money he'd made, he published on his own another story that summer and made back the money he'd lost.

"I guess that means I won in the end, at least in a financial sense," he has said. "But in my heart I stayed ashamed. I kept hearing [the teacher] asking why I wanted to waste my talent, why I wanted to waste my time, why I wanted to write junk."

At the age of 13, King began to submit stories to science fiction magazines. In one of his favorites, an asteroid miner discovers a pink cube that oozes some viscous substance; the substance—the goo—backs him into his space-hut, breaching airlock after airlock until it gets him. His efforts earned him a collection of rejection slips, which he impaled, as trophies, on a nail he'd pounded into the bedroom wall. "By the time I was 14 (and shaving twice a week whether I needed to or not) the nail in my wall would no longer support all the weight of rejection slips impaled upon it," King remembered. "I replaced the nail with a spike and went on writing."

In the spring of 1962, King graduated from grammar school, first in his class of three students; high school was in Lisbon Falls, about six miles from Durham. The town couldn't afford a bus for the few Durham students of high-school age, so they hired a Lisbon taxi service to drive the students in an old limousine. King's grades were good but not spectacular. He earned a B average, earning high grades in subjects that required writing but faring poorly in subjects like chemistry and physics. "My high school career was totally undistinguished. I was not at the top of my class, nor at the bottom," he remembered. "I had friends, but none of them were the big jocks or the student council guys or anything like that."

Despite undistinguishing academics, King did possess two distinguishing traits—he loved to read, and he loved to write. He kept paperbacks in his pocket, often reading as he walked between classes. He lumped books into two categories—"Gotta Reads" for those books that were assigned, and "Wanna Reads" for those authors he enjoyed reading—Ed McBain, Ray Bradbury, John D. MacDonald, Shirley Jackson, Ken Kesey, and Jack London. King's voracious reading made him ever more eager to write.

As a sophomore, King published *The Village Vomit*, a parody of the school newspaper, lampooning some of his teachers. "At the close of school I was for the second time in my student career summoned to the office on account of something I had written," he recalls. As punishment for his publication, King had to spend one week in detention hall and make apologies to several teachers, which, he says, "were warranted, but . . . tasted like dog-dirt in my mouth." Meanwhile, the school's guidance counselor decided King needed a more constructive outlet for his creative energies. He arranged with the editor of the town's small weekly newspaper for King to cover sports.

King skulked reluctantly into the newspaper office. The newspaper's editor, John Gould, gave King a roll of yellow paper, promised him a half-cent a word, and sent him off to cover a basketball game. King returned with two stories, a straight story about the game and a feature story about the game's hero. The first story Gould tossed into the trash. King recalls:

> Then he started in on the feature piece with a large black pen and taught me all I ever needed to know about my craft. When Gould finished marking up my copy . . . he looked up and must have seen something on my face. I think he must have thought it was horror, but it was not: It was revelation. "I only took out the bad parts, you know," he said. "Most of it's pretty good."
>
> "I know," I said, meaning both things. Yes, most of it was good, and yes, he had only taken out the bad parts. "I won't do it again."
>
> "If that's true," he said, "you'll never have to work again. You can do this for a living." Then he threw back his head and laughed.

King continued to write fiction. In 1963, he self-published *People, Places and Things* on his brother's mimeograph. The book, a collection of writings by King and his friend Chris, was written on King's old typewriter, which had missing letters that King had to pencil in. Even at that early stage, he was writing horror, with stories like "Hotel at the End of the Road," "The Strange," and "The Other Side of the Fog."

Meanwhile, he kept submitting stories to magazines, and his first publication came in 1965. He wrote "I Was a Teenage Grave Robber," which appeared in *Comics Review*. Throughout high school, King kept several close friends, played left tackle on the football team, and played rhythm guitar in a rock band. His band, the Mule-Spinners, played at the senior prom.

King was acutely aware of the caste system at school, and he knew that he wasn't in the upper echelons of it:

> I had friends and all that, but I often felt unhappy and different, estranged from other kids my age. I was a fat kid—husky was the euphemism they used in the clothing store—and pretty poorly coordinated, always the last picked when we chose teams.
>
> At times, particularly in my teens, I felt violent, as if I wanted to lash out at the world, but that rage I kept hidden. That was a secret place in myself I wouldn't reveal to anyone else.

These feelings formed the basis of what has been called his first mature story, although he didn't complete it until years later. The summer after he graduated, King began "Getting It On," a story that explores the mind of a boy whose rage drives him to hold his classmates hostage. The story marked the beginning of King's life-long exploration of the fears lurking in ordinary people and how they play out in extraordinary circumstances.

CAMPUS INSTITUTION

King's mother had always insisted that he would go to college. "You're not going to punch a time clock all your life," she would say. In the fall of 1966, King arrived at the University of Maine at Orono, with a scholarship that covered his tuition and books. He later wrote in the campus newspaper:

> There I was, all alone in Room 203 of Gannett Hall, clean-shaven, neatly dressed, and as green as apples in August. Outside on the grass by Gannett and Androscoggin Hall there were more people playing football than there were in my home town. My few belongings looked pitifully un-collegiate. The room looked mass-produced. I was quite sure my roommate would turn out to be some kind of a freako, or even worse, hopelessly more "with it" than I.

Again King used his writing to forge a world apart from his loneliness and alienation. His freshman composition instructor noticed his talent from the start. "Steve was a nice kid, a good student, but never had a lot of social confidence," Jim Bishop has said. "Even then, though, he saw himself as a famous writer and thought he could make money at it. Steve was writing continuously, industriously, and diligently. He was amiable, resilient, and created his own world."

During his freshman year, King became aware of the student-organized "walkathons" that served as fundraisers for charitable concerns. He began to wonder what would happen if this walkathon idea went too far. With that, he began writing the story of a nation whose teenage boys are celebrated in a walk in which only one can finish alive. He asked a professor to take a look at *The Long Walk*, and the professor's wife picked up the manuscript and couldn't stop reading. Soon *The Long Walk* had made the rounds of the English department, to much acclaim. King submitted the story to a first-novel competition with high hopes, and it was rejected with a form letter.

By the beginning of his sophomore year, King had collected another stack of rejections. Then, in the fall, King sold his first story. *Startling Mystery Stories* sent him his first professional check—for $35. "I've cashed many bigger since then," King said years later, "but none gave me more satisfaction; someone had finally paid me some real money for something I had found in my head."

In that year King published two stories in the college literary magazine, *Ubris*. Again he found inspiration in his isolation from his peers. In "Cain Rose Up" he told the story of a student who snaps under pressure and shoots students from a window in his dormitory. The story was different from the magazine's usual prose, and King began to make a name for himself on campus as a writer whose images were raw and real. He also wrote another novel that year, but he could not place it with a publisher.

As King explored creative writing through coursework, he began his struggle with the more accepted—academic—definition of *literature*. It was a struggle that he would maintain throughout his career. In defining literature, King's professor of creative writing stressed a writer's duty to form themes and symbolism intentionally into his work. These, he said, were the marks of literary fiction; driving plots and motivated characters were all well and good, but this was not enough to ensure a work's transposition from the category of popular fiction to the realm of literature. He concluded that only literature was worth reading, studying, or teaching.

King cringed at the distinctions. His writing had always been intuitive. He let his characters and the plot create a story without much thought to themes and symbolism and literary realms. The professor's views rankled King and reminded him of the shame he had felt when that earlier teacher had called his writing "junk."

As a junior King continued publishing in *Ubris*, once placing a story that he wrote in less than two hours on napkins in the cafeteria. He also worked on his third book. Early in the spring semester of 1969 he started a regular column in the *Maine Campus*, called "King's Garbage Truck", in which he reviewed movies and television programs, opined on controversies like the Vietnam War and birth control, and mused about baseball and girl-watching. King often appeared in the office to write his column only hours before the newspaper's firm Tuesday deadlines.

In the same year he placed his second paid story, also in *Startling Mystery Stories*. "Reaper's Image" earned King another $35.

As his confidence as a writer grew, King's confidence in his professors' definitions of literature and serious writing diminished. Horror writing, which began as gothic European tales of haunted castles in the 18th century, had become so popular that it was condemned as fiction for the masses, unworthy of serious attention. It was considered a medium in which for the talentless to rake in easy money.

King disagreed. He argued that popular fiction deserved more attention, and initiated running battles with several English professors. He argued that academia was sticking its head in the sand when it ignored popular fiction. He approached the university with a plan to teach a special seminar on popular American fiction. The project was controversial: undergraduates just did not teach other undergraduates. He pressed, and, with an established teacher as the class's official professor, King taught Popular Literature and Culture, the first seminar on the subject at the university and the first time an undergraduate had taught. He'd won a skirmish, but the battle over *literature* was far from over.

College was changing King. His ideas about literature were coalescing, even while his ideas about politics were undergoing radical transformation. King had come to college with a firm belief in the Republican Party. He'd worked on the campaign of Republican presidential candidate Barry Goldwater in 1964 and voted for Richard Nixon in 1968. He was convinced that those insolent young men burning their draft cards in protest of the Vietnam War were "yellow-bellies."

But he followed many of his fellow students into peace movement liberalism as he saw waves of young men dying in Vietnam and Nixon's presidency disintegrating. By his graduation, he had participated in several local peace marches; taken acid, peyote, and mescaline more than 60 times; and grown long hair. He proudly called himself "a scummy radical bastard."

Attendance on scholarship meant King slaved for every penny of spending money he had. During his four years at the university, he worked as a dishwasher, as a Little League coach, and as an attendant at a gas station. He was working in the university library when he met Tabitha Spruce. "Tabby looked like a waitress," he said, remembering the first time he saw her. "She came across—and still does—as a tough broad." Tabitha King remembers a friend pointing King out to her sometime before they met. He seemed imposing, already a campus institution known for his writing. Tabitha, who was majoring in history, also wrote. The two of them hit it off, as King remembers:

> We met when we were working in a library, and I fell in love with her during a poetry workshop in the fall of 1969, when I was a senior and Tabby was a junior. I fell in love with her partly because I understood what she was doing with her work. I fell because she understood what she was doing with it. I also fell because *she* was wearing a sexy black dress and silk stockings, the kind that hook with garters.

By his senior year, King had moved out of the dormitories and was living in a riverside cabin close to campus. He spent hours in front of his typewriter, using two fingers to type his stories. "The man in black fled across the desert and the gunslinger followed," he pecked out. Just before graduation, he finished *Sword in the Darkness*, the first book of *The Dark Tower* series on which his work continues today. But once again, none of the publishing houses wanted it. King would leave school with four unpublished novels and little hope of selling them.

King graduated in June of 1970 with a degree in English, a minor in speech, and a teacher's certification for secondary school. He was 22, stood six foot three inches, weighed 207 pounds, and was disillusioned. In his last "King's Garbage Truck" column, he wrote:

> (The future is) hazy, although either nuclear annihilation or environmental strangulation seemed to be definite possibilities. . . . If a speaker at his birth into the real world mentions "changing the world with the bright-eyed vigor of youth," this young man is apt to flip him the bird and walk out, as he does not feel very bright-eyed by this time: in fact, he feels about two thousand years old.

SAPPY GRINS AND BESTSELLERS

After graduation, King and Tabitha Spruce continued to date. By Christmas of that year, King wanted to spend the rest of his life with her, and on January 2, 1971 they were married. The ceremony was held at a Catholic church in honor of her religious background, and the reception in a Methodist church in honor of his.

With a glut of teachers in Maine, King couldn't find a teaching job. He went to work at another gas station, then at a laundromat for $60 a week while Tabitha finished college. The laundromat serviced local restaurants, which meant King cleaned a lot of tablecloths coated with lobster and clam. "By the time the tablecloths upon which these delicacies had been served reached me, they stank to high heavens and were often boiling with maggots," King remembered. "The maggots would try to crawl up your arms as you loaded the washers. . . . I thought I'd get used to them in time but I never did."

The couple had moved into a run-down apartment in Orono and struggled to pay the bills. King continued to write, sometimes during his lunch hour. By now he was regularly selling horror and suspense tales to men's magazines like *Adam*, *Swank*, and *Cavalier*, usually making $200 to $300 per publication.

Often the money came just in time. King was driving home around midnight one night with his car's tail pipe nearly falling off when he ran over a traffic cone. The pipe clattered to the road. Irked, King drove around town collecting the offending cones, planning to drop them off in front of the police station. A police officer stopped him and asked if the cones were his. They weren't, and King was given the choice of paying a $250 fine or spending 30 days in jail. A $250 check from *Adam* came just in time.

Desperate, King turned into a novel a story he had begun in high school. He sent *Getting It On* to Doubleday, where it landed on the desk of editor Bill Thompson. Thompson thought the book slow and claustrophobic, but he encouraged King to keep trying.

In the spring of 1971, Tabitha graduated with a degree in history, but the only job she could find was as a waitress at a donut shop in Bangor. Even with both Kings working, money was tight, especially when their first child, Naomi, was born. Their situation became more precarious with the birth of Joseph a year later.

Later in 1971, King secured a teaching position at Hampden Academy in Hermon, Maine, teaching six periods of high school English for $6,400 a year. He and Tabitha moved into a trailer in town. He had a knack for teaching, and the students liked him from the start. Even the administration was impressed with his approach. But each night when King came home with a stack of papers to grade and no time to write, he felt himself slipping:

> For the first time in my life, writing was *hard*. The problem was the teaching. I liked my coworkers and loved the kids—even the Beavis and Butt-Head types in Living with English could be interesting—but by most Friday afternoons I felt as if I'd spent the week with jumper cables clamped to my brain. If I ever came close to despairing about my future as a writer, it was then. I could see myself 30 years on, wearing the same shabby tweed coats with patches on the elbows, potbelly rolling over my Gap khakis from too much beer. I'd have a cigarette cough from too many packs of Pall Malls, thicker glasses, more dandruff, and in my desk drawer, six or seven unfinished manuscripts which I would take out and tinker with from time to time, usually when drunk.

In his furnace room office, in the little time he had between reading student papers and diapering babies, King finished his fifth novel, *The Running Man*. It was the story of a man who risks his life on a game show in order to provide for his wife and sick child. It was the story of King's fear that he would never make enough to take care of his family. When Thompson rejected this book too, King threw it in a drawer, where it would stay for almost a decade.

While still working at the laundry, King had started a short story inspired by a job he'd had in college cleaning a high school. One day while cleaning the girls' bathroom, he had noticed something peculiar:

> I looked around the locker room with the interest of a Muslim youth who for some reason finds himself deep within the women's quarters. It was the same as the boy's locker room, and yet completely different. There were no urinals, and there were two extra metal boxes on the tile walls—unmarked, and the wrong size for paper towels.

While he worked at the laundry, the memory returned, and King saw the opening scene. A shy, awkward girl experiences menarche while showering in the locker room and, ignorant of the process, thinks she is bleeding to death. The other girls tease her and throw tampons and napkins. King knew the girl's revenge would make a good story.

An article he had read pushed into his mind. The article had reported a phenomenon called telekinesis, the ability to move things with the mind, and that telekinesis seemed to be most prevalent in girls just reaching their first menstruation. "Pow!" King recalls. "Two unrelated ideas, adolescent cruelty and telekinesis, came together, and I had an idea."

It was soon after this that Tabitha rescued the manuscript of *Carrie* from the garbage and encouraged him to submit it. He did. Expecting another refusal to publish, he sank into a depression.

King had four rejections from Doubleday and only men's magazines to his credit. The telephone was disconnected; his seven-year-old car needed repair; the baby cried. King hardly found time to write. He remembered:

> I wish I could say today that I bravely shook my fist in the face of adversity and carried on undaunted, but I can't. I copped out to self-pity and anxiety and started drinking far too much and frittering money away on poker and bumper pool. You know the scene: it's Friday night and you cash your paycheck in the bar and start knocking them down, and before you know what's happened, you've pissed away half the food budget for that week. I'd wander around the crummy little living room of our trailer at three o'clock on a cold winter's morning with my teething nine-month-old son Joe slung over my shoulder, more often than not spitting up all over my shirt, and I'd try to figure out how and why I'd ever committed myself to that particular lunatic asylum. . . . and I'd say to myself, "Face it; you're going to be teaching . . . high school kids for the rest of your life." I don't know what would have happened to my marriage and my sanity if it hadn't been for the totally unexpected news, in 1973, that Doubleday had accepted *Carrie*, which I had thought had very little chance of a sale.

When the contract arrived, King, his friend Chris, and Tabitha sat drinking beer in the living room, going over the contract clause by clause. When the papers were signed and the check arrived, King and Tabitha bought a new blue Pinto and moved into a second-story apartment in Bangor with a connected telephone.

King's elation was qualified by the illness of his mother, who was dying of cancer while he prepared *Carrie* for publication. King and his brother held her hands as she took her last breath. *Carrie* sold only 13,000 copies in hardcover, and the reviews were sparse. Writing for the May 26, 1974 issue of *The New York Times*, though, Newgate Callendar foreshadowed King's future, calling the work "extraordinary," "exceedingly well-written," and "guaranteed to give you a chill."

As a paperback, the book fared far better, selling 2.5 million copies. Hollywood released Bryan De Palma's film version, starring Sissy Spacek, Piper Laurie, Amy Irving, and John Travolta, in 1976. King had exploded onto the scene of popular culture.

With his career as a novelist underway, King quit teaching:

> Hell, our lives changed so quickly that for more than a year afterward, we walked around with big, sappy grins on our faces, hardly daring to believe we were out of that trap for good. It was a great feeling of liberation, because at last I was free to quit teaching and fulfill what I believe is my only function in life: to write books. Good, bad or indifferent books, that's for others to decide; for me, it's enough just to write.

Just before selling *Carrie*, King had been teaching *Dracula* to his students, and he had begun to explore the idea of Dracula in a small town in Maine. *Salem's Lot* resulted. With one successful novel under his belt, he had no trouble finding a publisher this time. And the timing could not have been more fortunate: the paperback edition came out just before *Carrie* was released in theaters. The movie helped to sell the book, and Hollywood saw the prospect of another hit. The story would eventually be made into a two-part made-for-television movie, which would air in 1979.

While most genre writers tended to develop a devoted following of like-minded readers, King was drawing readers who didn't usually buy horror. He was attracting a mainstream audience, and he had reached the top of the *New York Times* bestseller list for paperback fiction.

Within two years, the Kings' life had changed. There would be no drudgery in a laundry, no more slogging through grammar with high school students, and no more late nights typing in the furnace room. King now had the luxury of developing his own writing routine, a routine that hasn't changed much in decades.

He works two or three hours each morning, seven days a week. He usually begins the day with a walk, then heads for his office to write six pages of new material. Later in the afternoon, he often spends a couple of hours rewriting or attending to the administrative aspects of his career. He rarely deviates: even if one of his children "fell down the stairs and broke his neck," he says, "I'd say, 'Fine, go take him to the emergency room, and let me finish this page.'" He sees writing as a craft, something worked on diligently, regularly. It's a job for him, albeit one that pays him handsomely and keeps him sane. He never waits for inspiration. "People think the muse is a literary character," King says, "some cute little pudgy devil who floats around the head of the creative person sprinkling fairy dust. Well, mine's a guy with a flattop in coveralls who looks like Jack Webb and says, 'All right, you son of a bitch, time to get to work.'"

For his third book, King wanted a change of scene. "I think it's time to set a book somewhere else," he told Tabitha. "This looks like it's going to be a career and not a hobby."

Tabitha lugged out a road atlas, tied a handkerchief over King's eyes, and told him to point. His finger jabbed at Colorado, close to Boulder. In 1974, the Kings packed up and drove west. King found Colorado's mountains and howling wind perfect for the story he had in mind, one of a psychic boy. But when he sat down at his typewriter, the story refused to come.

Frustrated, the couple took decided to spend a weekend away at a nearby mountain retreat that a friend had recommended. They arrived at the Stanley Hotel to find everyone else leaving; it was the last day of the season. Rolled up fire hoses lined the long corridors, eerie with silence. Dining room chairs were overturned on tables. After dinner, King had a drink by himself at the bar, and he got lost in a maze of corridors. When he found his room, he pushed the bathroom door open and saw the claw-footed bathtub with a pink shower curtain drawn tightly closed. He began to fantasize about someone dying in that bathtub. "By then, whatever it is that makes you want to make things up . . . was turned on," King said. "I was scared, but I loved it."

He took the psychic boy and put him in the fictional Overlook Hotel with parents whose marriage was crumbling. In six weeks, he had written *The Shining*.

King didn't linger in Boulder, which he found rife with yuppies. In the summer of 1975, the family moved back to Maine, where he settled in to polish *The Shining*. The father in the book loses touch with his sanity, driven over the edge partly by evil and partly by alcoholism. Suddenly King saw he was writing about himself. He said:

> I spent the first 12 years of my married life assuring myself that I just liked to drink. I also employed the Hemingway Defense. . . . The Hemingway Defense goes something like this: as a writer, I am a very sensitive fellow, but I am also a man, and real men don't give in to their sensitivities. Only sissy-men do that. Therefore I drink. How else can I face the existential horror of it all and continue to work? Besides, come on, I can handle it. A real man always can.

So King set about handling it. He'd be careful, he told himself. He'd keep it under control. He would manage to do this for almost 10 years.

When *The Shining* came out in 1977, King had his first best-selling hardback. The book's jacket flap called King "the undisputed master of the modern horror story". Soon, books promoted themselves as "in the tradition of Stephen King."

British film director Stanley Kubrick was interested in producing a horror film and saw *The Shining* as the perfect vehicle. Still new to fame and fortune, King remembers the surreal conversations with Hollywood over the making of the film:

> We had lunch at the Waldorf with people who bought the movie rights to *The Shining*. We sat in leather chairs. . . . The waiters were all French. They glide over to you. And we sat around the table talking seriously about people to play roles in the movie. "What do you think about Robert De Niro for the father?" somebody says. Somebody else says, "I think Jack Nicholson would be terrific." And I say, "Don't you think Nicholson is too old for the part?" And so it goes. We're tossing around these names from the fan magazines—except it's for real. The check comes and it's $140.00 without drinks, and somebody picks it up without batting an eye.

In 1980, the film version of *The Shining* was released. With Kubrick, an $18 million budget, and Jack Nicholson in the lead, King had high hopes. Moviegoers loved the result. Even decades later, *The Shining* still has a cult following that has made it one of the most popular horror films of all time.

King, however, was disappointed in Kubrick's vision:

> He used to make transatlantic calls to me from England at odd hours of the day and night, and I remember once he rang up at seven in the morning and asked, "Do you believe in God?" I wiped the shaving cream away from my mouth, thought a minute and said, "Yeah, I think so." Kubrick replied, "No, I don't think there is a God," and hung up. Not that religion has to be involved in horror, but a visceral skeptic such as Kubrick just couldn't grasp the sheer inhuman evil of the Overlook Hotel. So he looked, instead, for evil in the characters and made the film into a domestic tragedy with only vaguely supernatural overtones. That was the basic flaw: because he couldn't believe, he couldn't make the film believable to others.

King had liked the previous two movie versions of his books. *Carrie* had even been more stylish and dense than the book, he thought.

But in the next few years, a steady flow of King novels would become B-movies. Part of the problem was that directors were used to making films that appealed to a teenage audience, which is believed to want cheap thrills and rivers of blood. King's horror was more psychological, harder to access:

> It's between the lines in the books. It's whatever it is, it's whatever flavor that readers come to expect and they come to want, it's the sort of thing that they come to crave. It's the only reason they go back to buy more. . . . And it's the same reason they don't go to the movies; they say, "Ah, it's just another shitty adaptation of a King book."

GETTING IT ALL

When, in 1977, King was ready to publish his fourth book, *Rage* (which he had originally written and failed to publish several years before under the title *Getting It On*), Doubleday worried that a glut of King books would turn readers off. King wondered what would happen if his now famous writing appeared under another name. Would it still make the bestseller lists? Would it attract movie offers? Would anyone notice the similarities in style? King published *Rage* under the pseudonym Richard Bachman.

King kept his assumed name secret; only the editor and an attorney handling the contract knew. To keep up the ruse, King asked that the books be published with plain covers and without a lot of promotion. When the copyright was filed at the Library of Congress, though, the paperwork had Stephen King's name on it. The error would go unnoticed for seven years, and Bachman would become one of the best-kept secrets in publishing history. Critics and readers ignored *Rage*.

That fall, King had an English ghost story on his mind. He, Tabitha, Naomi, Joe, and newborn Owen packed up for England, planning to stay of one year. They placed an advertisement in *The Fleet News*: "Wanted, a draughty Victorian house in the country with dark attic and creaking floorboards, preferably haunted."

Despite the name of its location, the house they rented at Mourlands, Fleet Hants, was not haunted. And it wasn't inspiring King with his ghost story. Instead, King kept thinking of an article he'd read about a little kid who'd been killed by a Saint Bernard. That story mingled in his imagination with an experience he'd had taking his motorcycle to a mechanic on the outskirts of town. The motorcycle had died in the mechanic's driveway just as a giant growling Saint Bernard had appeared. The mechanic emerged and told King not to worry. When the dog kept growling, the mechanic hit it on the rump with a socket wrench. King wondered what would have happened if the mechanic had not been present.

While in England, King and Tabitha went to dinner at the home of Peter Straub, who had written the wildly popular *Ghost Story*. The two authors had become acquainted after King's writing of a bit for Peter's book. Peter had written to thank him. King had written back, saying he was coming for a visit, during which the two hit it off. After dinner, King and Straub talked about writing a novel together. Both had projects and contracts to fulfill, however, so they postponed the realization of their idea.

King spent the remainder of his time in England working on *Cujo*, the story of a boy and his mother trapped in their car by a rabid Saint Bernard. King stayed in England only three months; by the end of the year, the Kings were back in Maine for good. With its isolated towns and plain, working-class folks, Maine was all the inspiration King needed. They bought a house on a lake near Center Lovell, where the family found some protection against the growing stream of fans, reporters, and appearance requests.

In that spring, King accepted an invitation to teach courses in literature creative writing at his alma mater, the University of Maine at Orono. It would be fun to teach college classes, King thought. He wouldn't have to plow through mundane details like grammar as he'd done while teaching high school.

While he taught, he thought about a news story he'd read detailing an accident at a chemical/biological warfare station in Utah. Sheep had died, and had the wind shifted residents of Salt Lake City would have died, too. In a nihilistic mood, King began to wonder what would happen if a super-flu virus swept across the globe.

The first version of *The Stand* was a 1,200-page epic, exploring the battle between good and evil in a nation whose population had been decimated by the flu. King whittled it to 800 pages after his publisher's balking at the printing costs. He promised himself to restore the cuts someday and publish it again.

As early as King's second novel, Bill Thompson of Doubleday had worried that King would typecast himself if he kept writing horror. King explained in response that he had to write what came to him, and so far this had been horror. Besides, King said, contrary to the view of the literary elite, horror did have serious overtones. The edges of scientific knowledge—pyrokinesis, extrasensory perception, telekinesis—drew him. He said:

> I wouldn't say I believe in them. The scientific verdict's still out on most of those things, and they're certainly nothing to accept

as an article of faith. But I don't think we should dismiss them out of hand just because we can't as yet understand how and why they operate and according to what rules. . . .There's a lot of mystery in the world, a lot of dark, shadowy corners we haven't explored yet. We shouldn't be too smug about dismissing out of hand everything we can't understand. The dark can have teeth, man!

The Stand, then, was a turning point. Until then King had written horror, but the epic tale was an amalgamation of science fiction, horror and fantasy. It defied classification.

King's books kept selling, and his audience grew slightly with each success. In 1978 he published *The Dead Zone*, *The Long Walk* (as Richard Bachman), and *Firestarter*. Both King books sold phenomenally well. Bachman's, again, went unnoticed.

In the summer of 1980, the Kings bought a historic home in Bangor, Maine, some 160 miles northeast of Center Lovell, retaining the first house for occasional use. Bangor was an ideal town for King. It had a major airport, a university with an excellent library, bookstores, and a theater. It was a proletarian town, where King's informal style of dress fit right in. The town would be the inspiration for the fictional town of Derry in many of King's books over the next few years.

The 23-room house, built in 1856 and of the Italianate style, *looks* like a horror writer's lair. It is surrounded with a black iron fence of spider webs and two guarding bats. King's office, complete with a stained-glass panel of bats in flight and a hidden stairway leading down to the indoor swimming pool, is in the stable's loft.

The house is even haunted, King says, by the spirit of an old man named Conquest, who died in the parlor decades ago. "I've never seen the old duffer, but sometimes when I'm working late at night, I get a distinctly uneasy feeling that I'm not alone," King says. "I wish he'd show himself; maybe we could get in some cribbage. Nobody in my generation will play with me." Neither Tabitha nor the King children feel the same cold shiver. King says:

Actually, I can't understand my own family sometimes. I won't sleep without a light on in the room and, needless to say, I'm very careful to see that the blankets are tucked tight under my legs so I won't wake up in the middle of the night with a clammy hand clutching my ankle. But when Tabby and I were first married, it was summer and she'd be sleeping starkers and I'd be lying there with the sheets pulled up to my eyes and she'd say, "Why are you sleeping in that crazy way?" And I tried to explain that it was just safer that way, but I'm not sure she really understood. And now she's done something else I'm not very happy with: she's added this big fluffy flounce around the bottom of our double bed, which means that before you go to sleep, when you want to check what's hiding under there, you have to flip up that flounce and poke your nose right in. And it's too close, man; something could claw your face right off before you spotted it. But Tabby just doesn't appreciate my point of view. . . .

But it's not only Tabby who doesn't understand; I'm disturbed by the attitude of my kids, too. I mean, I suffer a bit from insomnia, and every night, I'll check them in their beds to see that they're still breathing, and my two oldest, Naomi and Joe, will always tell me, "Be sure to turn off the light and close the door when you leave, Daddy." Turn off the light! Close the door! How can they face it? I mean, my God, anything could be in their room, crouched inside their closet, coiled under their bed, just waiting to slither out, pounce on them and sink its talons into them! Those things can't stand the light, you know, but the darkness is dangerous! But try telling that to my kids. I hope there's nothing wrong with them.

In 1981 and 1982, readers snapped up *Cujo* and *Different Seasons*, a collection of novellas. They pored over King's first non-fiction work, *Danse Macabre*, a serious look at the horror genre. Two Bachman books, *Roadwork* and *The Running Man*, the latter released after a decade's shelving, were again mostly unread.

In 1982, King also published the first book of the epic fantasy he'd begun in college, *The Dark Tower*, a series that he estimates will eventually include, in total, eight books. At first King published the novel only in a limited edition advertised in fantasy magazines—a thank you to the fantasy community that had nurtured his early career. But when word got out, demand ran so high that he was forced to publish it, and all future *Dark Tower* books, traditionally.

By this time, all King's movies had been adaptations of his books. Also in 1982, though, he wrote his first original screenplay, *Creepshow*. This was a series of five vignettes based on the horror comics of the 1950s, a subgenre King knew intimately. King tried acting for the first time, playing bumpkin Jordy Verrill, who is slowly colonized by a plant. King's son Joe also acted in the film, playing a young comic collector who begins the story.

The work was grueling—"Near the end of 'Jordy,'" King remembered, "I was in a chair for six hours a day getting this Astroturf stuff put all over my body."—but King created a few bright spots. Once he slipped on a fungi-covered mold of his tongue and headed off the set:

> There was a shopping mall next door, and I went in there one day wearing this thing into some department store where this salesgirl came up and said, "Can I help you?" I stuck out my tongue and went "Bleeeahhh!" and she went "Yaaaaaahhhhhh!!" She went bullshit, called the mall cop and everything, but it was worth it, it was so funny.

When the film came out, just before Halloween in 1982, King wasn't thrilled with either his performance or the film as a whole. But he did get his first inside look at acting and directing—a lesson he would find valuable later. King continued to play cameo roles in his movies: including a truck driver (*Creepshow 2*), a bus driver (*Golden Years*), a minister (*Pet Sematary*), a cemetery caretaker (*Sleepwalkers*), a lawyer (*Storm of the Century*), a doctor (*Thinner*), and several others.

In 1983, two more King books came out, both of which would be adapted on film. *Christine* told the story of a boy and his haunted 1958 Plymouth Fury. The story was born of King's fascination with teenage culture and the car's status as an American rite of passage. As King has said, "The car is the way the journey is made."

The second book that year scared King more than any he had written. He'd finished a draft four years earlier, but he had found it too terrifying to continue. *Pet Sematary* dealt with losing the most precious thing in his life—his children.

Being a father wasn't easy for King. He had learned things about himself that he didn't want to know:

> I grew up without a father. I didn't have any experience in my own home, so when I got married and had kids, I had to fall back on the real role model of young American men, which is television.
>
> I thought I knew what a dad was. Fathers on TV were always cool. They had it together. Dad even wore a tie to the dinner table.
>
> The first time I realized that parents are not always good was when the kid wouldn't stop crying in the middle of the night. I was getting up to get the kid a bottle, and somewhere in the back

of my mind, in some sewer back there, an alligator stirs . . . make it stop crying. You know how to do it—use the pillow.

These were shocking, unpleasant emotions for me to discover in myself. . . . I was brought face-to-face with the idea that I was not always good in my motivations.

The idea for *Pet Sematary* began after Naomi's cat, Smucky, was killed by a car on Thanksgiving. They buried the cat in a local pet graveyard the neighborhood kids had created. King noticed the sign the kids had made, complete with misspellings—Pet Sematary. He wondered what would happen if a cat came back to life. Three days after Smucky's funeral, King caught hold of two-year-old Owen just as he ran into the road. What would happen, he wondered, if a human came back?

When it finally came out, *Pet Sematary* became known as King's most terrifying book. It turned out that King's worst fear—that his child might die—was universal. He said:

We can't cope with it; it'll drive us crazy. For me, the fact that it doesn't is one of the really marvelous things in human existence, and probably also one of the true signs of God's grace on the face of this earth. . . . At the same time, we have to prepare for it in some way; we have to experience all the possibilities. And so, for a lot of us, one of the ways we do it is take a worst-case analysis. We write about it; we read about it.

King worked at being a good father. He had his imagination, his television role models, Tabitha, and the luxury of working from home. He used them to be the kind of father he wished he'd had. He took his children to movies and to ball games; he coached Little League. And he saw the world afresh through their eyes—experiences he would use again and again in his books, as child characters would confront evil and horror with their naïve innocence. "It's a trip," King said. "It's like being in a time machine, too. You go back."

By now King's following was among the largest in the country. Readers devoured his books as fast as he wrote them, eager to share his horrific visions, eager to see themselves in the situations he creates. King begins with common characters engaged in common life—the convenience store, the local high school, the ordinary trappings of the ordinary day—and then forces them to confront universal fears. As the author himself puts it: "First you create people that you want to live, then you put them into the cooker."

For King, fear exists in three varieties. First there's revulsion, the gory material usually considered the lowest form the medium can assume. Next comes horror, the fear of something physical the writer describes, a fear evoked by an external source. At the top of the hierarchy is terror, the fear of the unseen, unleashed by a reader's own imagination. In King's words:

> Naturally, I'll try to terrify you first, and if that doesn't work, I'll try to horrify you, and if I can't make it there, I'll try to gross you out. I'm not proud; I'll give you a sandwich squirming with bugs or shove your hand into the maggot-churning innards of a long-dead woodchuck. I'll do anything it takes; I'll go to any lengths, I'll geek a rat if I have to—I've geeked plenty of them in my time. After all, as Oscar Wilde said, nothing succeeds like excess. So if somebody wakes up screaming because of what I wrote, I'm delighted. If he merely tosses his cookies, it's still a victory but on a lesser scale. I suppose the ultimate triumph would be to have somebody drop dead of a heart attack, literally scared to death. I'd say, "Gee, that's a shame," and I'd mean it, but part of me would be thinking, "Jesus, that really worked!"

For some readers, the technique has worked too well. In Florida, an allusion to *The Shining* was made in writing *REDRUM*—that is, *murder* spelled backward—on the walls of a murder scene. In Boston, a man butchered a woman using kitchen implements in imitation, police speculated, of a scene in *Carrie*. In Baltimore, a woman reading at a bus stop knifed to death a would-be mugger. When reporters asked her what she'd been reading, she proudly held up *The Stand*. Asked whether he feels responsible for these events, King said:

> Evil is basically stupid and unimaginative and doesn't need creative inspiration from me or anybody else. But despite know-ing all that rationally, I have to admit that it is unsettling to feel that I could be linked in any way, however tenuous, to somebody else's murder. So if I sound defensive, it's because I am.

Alone in the house at Center Lovell in 1983, as a northeastern wind blew snow across the frozen lake, King sat in front of the wood stove with a yellow legal pad and a cold beer and wrote 13 pages of *The Napkins*. The story was for one person—his daughter, Naomi. "Although I had written 13 novels by the time my daughter had attained an equal number of years," he recalls, "she hadn't read any of them. She's made it clear that she loves me, but has very little interest in my vampires, ghoulies and slushy crawling things." By the end of the year, King gave the book, later retitled *The Eyes of the Dragon*, to his daughter.

King says she began reading "with a marked lack of enthusiasm" but soon the story "kidnapped her". When she finished, she told her father the only thing she didn't like about the story was that it had to end. King basks: "That, my friends, is a writer's favorite song, I think." Four years later, in 1987, an illustrated version of *The Eyes of the Dragon* in hardcover would sell a phenomenal 525,000 copies in its first year.

That year would also see the second installment of another of King's nontraditional writing projects. The previous Christmas, after deciding Christmas cards were too impersonal, he had begun a story just for the 200 people on his Christmas card list. The first episode of *The Plant* was published by his own company, Philtrum Press, and bound in a little book. In 1987, he continued the story.

TRIUMPH AND TRIALS

In 1984, what had begun as a dinner conversation with writer Peter Straub resulted in the collaborative work *The Talisman*. Both authors knew that collaboration was rare. "I was intensely curious to see the result," King said. "Working together was like that ad where one guy says, 'You got chocolate on my peanut butter,' and the other guy says, 'You got peanut butter on my chocolate,' and they end up saying, 'Hey! This tastes pretty good.'"

King and Straub got together to write the novel's beginning and ending. For the middle, each writer worked on a section for a few weeks and then sent it electronically to the other.

The fantasy about a 12-year-old boy's saga in a world filled with werewolves and killer trees quickly became a bestseller. The combination mixed King's popular appeal with Straub's more literary reputation. Even with such different styles, though, most people weren't able to tell who wrote which parts. King and Straub agreed to keep the secret.

Meanwhile, Richard Bachman's secret was cracking. When King, as Bachman, put out *Thinner* in November of 1984, the book came complete with a dust-jacket picture of the supposed author, a middle-aged, balding dairy farmer from New Hampshire. Even the dedication "To my wife, Claudia Inez Bachman," helped to maintain the charade. Unlike the previous four Bachman books, though, which King had written before his rise to fame, *Thinner* was a recent creation and read like a familiar King novel.

Early in 1984, two dealers of fantasy books who had read advance copies declared that Bachman was King. Then, a teacher reviewing King novels for a Colorado newspaper wrote about odd similarities between the two authors—same publisher, both from New England, both creating stories set in Maine. Within the fantasy community, the pseudonym became an open secret. King had even given his readers a hint: In the book, one character tells another, "You were starting to sound a little like a Stephen King novel for a while there. . . ."

But the general public still didn't know. Then, in January of 1985, a bookstore clerk in Washington, D.C. wrote to King, enclosing a copy of the copyright registration to *Rage*, which had mistakenly used King's real name. Within days the story broke in newspapers and television shows nationwide.

A week later, *Thinner* hit the bestseller list. With Bachman as its author, the book had sold 28,000 copies; with King as author it sold another 280,000 copies in no time at all. That, King said, is not good news for the hundreds of great but unknown writers in America—or for the millions of readers who will never meet with their works.

Readers rushed to the stores to buy all four Bachman books, but only *Thinner* and *The Running Man* were still in print. Soon, all available copies were gone. People bought King's books no matter how many came out at once, flying in the face of the publishing axiom that readers don't want too many books by the same author on their nightstands at one time. To satisfy readers, King's publisher reissued all four Bachman books in one edition that fall.

In the mid-1980s, King movies appeared from Hollywood regularly—but with irregular results. *Cat's Eye*, a collection of three vignettes adapted from King's short stories, and *Silver Bullet*, based on a King specialty publication, opened in theaters in 1985, but neither captured the power of King's writing. Fortunately, *Stand By Me* was in production that year. Based on King's short story "The Body", this film would be directed not by a director known for his work in horror, but rather by Rob Reiner, who was known for his serious dramas. While Reiner worked to translate "The Body" onto film, King gave filmmaking a try himself.

Earlier in 1985, he had written a screenplay based on his short story "Trucks". King hoped he could change the public's mind about his films. "A lot of people have made movies out of my stories," King explained, " . . . but I thought it was time I took a crack at doing Stephen King. After all, if you want it done right, you have to do it yourself."

Between July and October, King worked in Wilmington, North Carolina, directing the $10 million production of *Maximum Overdrive*. Waking at 6 A.M., King would ride his motorcycle to the set, usually stopping at a fast-food restaurant for breakfast. All day, he'd guide the shooting through sticky heat. If he was uncertain how a shot should go, dozens of people had to wait for him to figure it out. After the daily wrap-up, King would review the day's shooting, returning to his rented house with a fast-food dinner at 8:30 P.M. For all this King earned $70,000—not the money he was used to making for the work of three months. "I didn't care for it at all," King remembered. "I had to work. I wasn't used to working. I hadn't worked in 12 years."

From a critical standpoint, the results were not worth King's indifference. When *Maximum Overdrive* was released, critics panned King's directorial debut. The film was extremely violent, and scenes had to be cut to reduce the MPAA's rating of it from X to R. In fact, it seemed to be more a shocker about being crushed by large vehicles than an exploration of the idea of machines taking over human lives.

Stand By Me was not promoted as a King movie when it opened in 1986. It began modestly, with advertising in only 16 theaters. But word of mouth quickly made it the surprise hit of the season. *Stand By Me* remains one of the best and most faithful adaptations of King's writing.

This wouldn't last. The next year's *The Running Man*, starring Arnold Schwarzenegger, was another gore-based adaptation far from the tone of King's work. *Pet Sematary* (1988) was an improvement—King had written the screenplay and persuaded Hollywood to shoot the film in Maine—but still the black terror of the book faded to gray on film.

By this time, King had become more than a best-selling author. He was a brand name. Everything he wrote sold easily. He was recognized everywhere he went. "I have grown into a Bestsellasaurus Rex—a big, stumbling book-beast that is loved when it shits money and hated when it tramples houses," King said. "I started out as a storyteller; along the way I became an economic force." The fame was both wonderful and horrifying:

> The occupational hazard of the successful writer in America is that once you begin to be successful, then you have to avoid being gobbled up. America has developed this sort of cannibalistic cult of celebrity, where first you set the guy up, and then you eat him. It happened to John Lennon; it has happened to a lot of rock stars. But I wish to avoid being eaten. I don't want to be anybody's lunch.

King had given up attending conferences because he was often mobbed. He kept his phone number unlisted and guarded both his writing and family time by hiring secretaries to handle his correspondence. King often encapsulates his experience of fame in a single story: He entered a bathroom stall at a swank restaurant; there were no doors on the stalls, and a man came up to him as he sat and asked him to sign an autograph. He did.

It was not long before he began to wonder what would happen if a fan's enthusiasm were carried to extremes. What if a fan really did try to gobble him up? In *Misery*, he created a fan who not only captured her favorite writer but forced him to write just what she wanted to read. True to form, King tapped into a fear of his own: this time, that fans of his horror writing wouldn't let his writing evolve into other genres.

When *Misery* came out in June 1987, many critics loved it, and some began to take King's work more seriously. But some readers and viewers lashed out, wondering indignantly whom he was calling maniacal and controlling. King replied:

> It's a 50-50 trade-off. I want you to read my book; you want to read my book. We get off even. They don't have a right to my life, but they take pieces of it just the same. When I went to look for videotapes this afternoon, there were a bunch [of fans] outside my house. I've had a lot of my life amputated already. It's like you're a Delco battery and someone's got a pair of jumpers on you all the time.

The upside of fame meant King had plenty of money and could live where he wanted, write what he wanted, and spend time with his family. He made a conscious effort to keep fame from degrading his working habits, his family life, or his character:

> There's really a simple and egotistical idea at the bottom of it all, one that has sustained creative artists since time immemorial. It's that feeling, when you're really into it, that "I'm great, they're going to love this, they're going to love me, I'll be rich and famous and never suffer—and never be constipated again." But that's only partly true. It's just life. Nothing really changes. I'll still be told by my wife, "King, we need a loaf of bread," and so I'll go out shopping. And if I forget, and come back instead with an idea that I tell her will make us $2 million, she'll still say, "King, I'm delighted, but we still need a loaf of bread."

It's Tabitha, King says, who has kept him from celebrity's pitfalls. Aside from their two luxury cars and their summer home in the White Mountains, the Kings look like an ordinary family.

King, at six feet four inches and 200 pounds, has blue eyes, thick glasses, and an infectious grin. His hair is jet-black and curls at his neck. He wears a full beard during the winter, shaving it off ritually at the start of the spring baseball season. He wears faded blue jeans and a work shirt. He pulls on a black leather jacket and scuffed boots when he goes out.

"The media," Tabitha wrote, "are frequently disappointed to discover an ordinary Yankee, size XL, drinking beer and watching baseball while his three children throw toys and his wife stews the checkbook."

When they were young, the kids wandered in and out of his study while King worked to the blast of rock music. They did ordinary things, like watch baseball or movies or go bowling or cross-country skiing.

Part of what kept their lives in order was King's decision to stay in Maine, far from the publishing glitter of New York or the movie glitz of Los Angeles. "Maine is far and away better for a couple of hicks like us," King said. "And it's better for the kids."

But Maine did have one flaw—its radio stations. Rock 'n' roll has been King's companion. When he writes and drives, he *needs* to hear Twisted Sister and AC/DC. Driving from Boston to Maine one day, he couldn't find anything resembling hard rock on the radio—so he bought a station. In 1982, a sleepy AM station suddenly began to blast speaker-blowing guitar riffs and screaming lyrics.

In 1995, King bought another radio station, this time an AM-FM combination, in Brewer, Maine. The FM station plays rock; the AM is a talk format. He interferes with day-to-day operations only enough to keep hard rock pounding along the airwaves.

By 1986, King had written several more books: *The Eyes of the Dragon*, the retitled story he had written for Naomi; *Skeleton Crew*, a collection of short stories; *It*, a tale of children who confront evil underneath their town and meet again as adults to destroy it. He had delivered the second book in *The Dark Tower* series and published *Misery* and *The Tommyknockers*.

His books were about the bloody, the horrific, and the evil; not surprisingly, he had become one of the most frequently banned authors in the country. *Carrie* had been challenged at a Las Vegas high school in 1975. It had been placed on a closed shelf in a high school library in Vermont because officials felt it may be harmful to young girls. *Cujo* had been regarded as "profane and sexually objectionable." Another school library removed it because it was "a bunch of garbage." *Firestarter* was challenged because of its language, sex, and violence. *The Shining* had been objected to as ridiculing Christianity. *Christine* was banned from all school libraries in one Alabama county because of its language and sex. *The Dead Zone* and *The Tommyknockers* had been pulled from school libraries in Jacksonville, Florida.

Because he was so often banned, organizers of Banned Book Week events at a library in Virginia Beach asked King to speak at their September 1986 lecture. He spoke to the crowd in his own relaxed way—with a beer in his hand. When a woman in the audience chastised King for his language, he defended himself:

I've written on love stories about a desperate people in desperate situations, and you know, it gets down to a point where you say to yourself, here's a guy who's building something in his garage, and he's all by himself and he's hammering a nail into the board and he misses that nail and he hits his thumb instead. And blood squirts out and everything. Now, does this guy say "Oh pickles"? Use your imagination.

I would just say to you as students who are supposed to be learning, as soon as that book is gone from the library, do not walk, run to your nearest public library or bookseller and find out what your elders don't want you to know because that's what you need to know. Don't let them bullshit you and don't let them guide your mind, because once that starts, it never stops.

Ironically, some listeners, incensed at his "public drinking and advocacy of sex and drugs," persuaded the mayor to ban his speech from appearing on a local cable show.

King had become involved in censorship issues before when, in 1977, a referendum was introduced in Maine to ban the sale of pornographic material. He spoke against the referendum on radio and wrote an opinion piece, arguing that such a law would take the responsibility of declining the sale from the hands of citizens and put it into the hands of the police and the courts. With 72 percent of the voters opposing it, the referendum failed.

Meanwhile, King's alcoholism had returned after a dormancy of ten years. He was deteriorating. By 1985, alcohol wasn't enough, and King began taking drugs. He remembered writing *The Tommyknockers* in 1986 with his heart sprinting and "cotton swabs stuck up [his] nose to stem the coke-induced bleeding."

Almost whenever he wrote, he drank alcohol and smoked marijuana. Finally, Tabitha stepped in:

> She organized an intervention group formed of family and friends, and I was treated to a kind of *This Is Your Life* in hell. Tabby began dumping a trash bag full of stuff from my office out on the rug: beer cans, cigarette butts, cocaine in gram bottles and cocaine in plastic Baggies, coke spoons caked with snot and blood, Valium, Xanax, bottles of Robitussin cough syrup and NyQuil cold medicine, even bottles of mouthwash. A year or so before, observing the rapidity with which huge bottles of Listerine were disappearing from the bathroom, Tabby asked me if I drank the stuff. I responded with self-righteous hauteur that I most

certainly did not. Nor did I. I drank the Scope instead. It was tastier, had that hint of mint.

She gave him a choice—enter a detoxification program or move out. She did not intend to watch, or to force the children to watch, King's slow suicide. King panicked. Would he be able to write without booze, without drugs? If the words stopped, could he keep going?

> Writing is necessary for my sanity. As a writer, I can externalize my fears and insecurities and night terrors on paper, which is what people pay shrinks a small fortune to do. In my case, they pay me for psychoanalyzing myself in print. And in the process, I'm able to "write myself sane," as that fine poet Anne Sexton put it. . . . All the rage and hate and frustration, all that's dangerous and sick and foul within me, I'm able to spew into my work. There are guys in padded cells all around the world who aren't so lucky.

Knowing that he was risking the basis on which he'd built his life and risking the work that held him together, King decided his marriage and family were more important. He would give up drinking and drugs, even if this meant sacrificing his writing. Fortunately, he never had to make that sacrifice. After his rehabilitation, King stayed sober and continued to write. He said:

> Some of the stuff that came out was tentative and flat, but at least it was there. I buried those unhappy, lackluster pages in the bottom drawer of my desk and got on to the next project. Little by little I found the beat again, and after that I found the joy again. I came back to my family with gratitude, and back to my work with relief—I came back to it the way folks come back to a summer cottage after a long winter, checking first to make sure nothing has been stolen or broken during the cold season. Nothing had been. It was still all there, still all whole. Once the pipes were thawed out and the electricity was turned back on, everything worked fine.

By March of 1989, King had finished his next book, *The Dark Half.* He originally planned to write it under both his own name and Bachman's, playing with the story's plot about a writer's pen name coming to life seeking vengeance after the writer decides abandon him.

While King continued to produce best-selling hard and paperback editions of his work, he also kept up his less-traditional publication. In 1989 he produced "My Pretty Pony," a limited-edition short story of only 280 copies, covered in stainless steel with an imbedded digital clock. Each book, about the triangular relationship among a child, his grandfather and his horse, sold for $2,200.

That year King also came out with *Dolan's Cadillac*. Only 1,200 copies, priced at between $100 and $250, were produced. In 1982, with his own Philtrum Press, King published *The Plant*, the serialized story he had originally written in lieu of Christmas cards. In 1984, Philtrum Press printed 1,250 copes of *The Eyes of the Dragon*, an edition signed and lavishly illustrated. They were sold by lottery for $120 each.

While King had been writing books by the dozen, Tabby had published her first novel in 1981. *The Small World* was followed two years later by *Caretakers*, *The Trap*, and, in 1988, *Pearl*. King admits to initial jealousy but says the feeling was short-lived:

> My reaction was like a little kid's: I felt like saying, "Hey, these are my toys; you can't play with them." But that soon changed to pride when I read the final manuscript and found she'd turned out a damned fine piece of work. I knew she had it in her, because Tabitha was a good poet and short-story writer when we started dating in my senior year at college, and she'd already won several prizes for her work. So I was able to come to terms with that childish possessiveness pretty quickly. Now, the first time she outsells me, that may be another story!

Perhaps this reciprocity is to be expected; King does name Tabitha as his own first reader, and he seems to prioritize her opinion in almost all literary matters:

> Someone—I can't remember who, for the life of me—once wrote that all novels are really letters aimed at one person. As it happens, I believe this. I think that every novelist has a single ideal reader, that at various points during the composition of a story, the writer is thinking, "I wonder what he/she will think when he/she reads this part?" For me that first reader is my wife, Tabitha.
>
> She and I may argue about many aspects of a book, and there have been times when I've gone against her judgment on subjective matters, but when she catches me in a goof, I know it,

and thank God I've got someone around who'll tell me my fly's unzipped before I go out in public that way.

CONFRONTING THE LITERATI

King began the 1990s with an old book, republishing, as he had promised himself when he had whittled the first version to a mere 800 pages, all 1,153 pages of *The Stand*. The additional pages added depth and drama missing from the first edition. *The Stand* quickly developed a cult following. The novel was one of King's favorites:

> *The Stand* was particularly fulfilling, because there I got a chance to scrub the whole human race and, man, it was fun! . . . After all the annihilation and suffering and despair, *The Stand* is inherently optimistic in that it depicts a gradual reassertion of humane values as mankind picks itself out of the ashes and ultimately restores the moral and ecological balance. Despite all the grisly scenes, the book is also a testament to the enduring human values of courage, kindness, friendship and love, and at the end it echoes Camus' remark, "Happiness, too, is inevitable."

One of the themes that run through King's books is that moral choices and people who have the courage to make them are the antidote to evil. It's this morality, King believes, that estranges him from the bulk of the literati, at least in part.

Since his undergraduate days, King has confronted the invisible line between literary writing and genre fiction. The traditional critical view classifies authors into two categories—the popular and the literary—perhaps forgetting that Shakespeare, Dickens, and Aeschylus all had enormous mass appeal in their times. King has often been excommunicated for the popularity of his work—which serious critics ignore, doctoral students don't study, and the highbrow either do not read or pretend not to read. *The Village Voice* has declared: "If you value wit, intelligence or insight, even if you're willing to settle for the slightest hint of good writing, all King's books are dismissible."

Although he professes not to mind this and is proud that his books are called the mind-candy of the masses, sometimes another desire peeks through:

> I'd like to win the National Book Award, the Pulitzer Prize, the Nobel Prize, I'd like to have someone write a *New York Times*

Book Review piece that says, "Hey, wait a minute guys, we made a mistake—this guy is one of the great writers of the 20th century." But it's not going to happen, for two reasons. One is I'm not the greatest writer of the 20th century, and the other is that once you sell a certain number of books, the people who think about "literature" stop thinking about you and assume that any writer who is popular across a wide spectrum has nothing to say. . . . I hear it in the voices of people from the literary journals where somebody will start by saying, "I don't read Stephen King," and they are really saying, "I don't lower myself."

Part of the reason King's books aren't considered literary is simply that he's been pigeon-holed as a horror writer. He has written many books far from horror, but even among his horror works King defends his work as different. He's not writing about gore and monsters, although these appear in abundance; he's writing about the struggle through evil to find good. Perhaps this is what the literary intelligentsia can't stand, King says:

I'm convinced that there exist absolute values of good and evil warring for supremacy in this universe—which is, of course, a basically religious viewpoint. And—what damns me even more in the eyes of the "enlightened" cognoscenti—I also believe that the traditional values of family, fidelity and personal honor have not all drowned and dissolved in the trendy California hot tub of the "me" generation. That puts me at odds with what is essentially an urban and liberal sensibility that equates all change with progress and wants to destroy all conventions, in literature as well as in society. . . . People like me really do irritate people like them, you know. In effect, they're saying, "What right do you have to entertain people? This is a serious world with a lot of serious problems. Let's sit around and pick scabs; that's art."

Another reason King cites for his failure to achieve literary-ness is his disagreement with the establishment about what makes a great book. Most say style; King says plot:

My idea about what a really good book is, is when the writer, whether he's alive or dead, suddenly reaches out of the page and grabs you by the throat and says, "You're mine, baby! You belong to me! Try to get away! You want to cook some dinner for your husband? Too bad! You want to go to bed? Tough shit! You're mine! You belong to me."

In recent years, however, some literary critics have been taking King's work more seriously. In 1990, his lengthy essay "Head Down" appeared in *The New Yorker*, one of the top forums for literary prose. The essay, about baseball, was included in an anthology of the year's best sports writing. In 1996, he won the prestigious O. Henry Award for a short story, "The Man in the Black Suit", also published in *The New Yorker*. Some of his competitors for the award have voiced dissatisfaction with a winner who scoffs the literary establishment.

Academia also has begun to notice King. As early as 1980, his alma mater began seriously collecting his work and papers. In 1996, the university held its first Stephen King conference. About 300 people attended, reading doctoral theses exploring his novels and participating in serious discussions of its literary merit. He was introduced as an author who was succeeding in spanning both mass and high culture. And this is what King says his work does: poke holes in the wall that divides genre writing from literary writing. "I have redefined the genre of horror-writing in this country," King said. "I'm not trying to say they're great books, mine, but for better or worse I have changed the genre."

But whether the literati notice him or not, nearly everyone else does. When *Publishers Weekly* compiled a list of the top 25 fiction bestsellers of the 1980s, King had written seven of them—almost one in four of the most-read books of the decade. King critic Michael Collings has said:

> I firmly believe that King speaks for our times; he touches on elements of American culture that are keystones to understanding ourselves. He is enormously popular—and scholars hate that. He writes for a popular audience—and academicians hate that. He tells stories for the sake of stories— and theorists hate that. He assumes the prose of a storyteller— and doctoral candidates hate that. On the other hand, he is being increasingly dissected by academics, many of whom seem more spurred by the "publish or perish" syndrome than by any real desire to understand the nature of horror—and fans hate that. But—kids read him.

For the most part, King is happy with that. When a reader finishes one of his books, King had rather she feel compelled to sleep with the light on than to ferret out symbolism.

As a celebrity writer, King had the chance to fulfill a fantasy dating to high school—to play in a real rock 'n' roll band. In May of 1992, at the Disneyland Hotel's main ballroom, King mounted the stage with several other famous writers, among them Robert Fulghum, Barbara Kingsolver, Amy Tan, and Dave Barry, as Garrison Keillor hosted "A Celebration for Free Expression: An Evening of Censored Classics." King played guitar and sang as a member of the Rock Bottom Remainders. Writers. Afterward, the Rock Bottom Remainders scooted over to the Cowboy Boogie bar for their first unplugged appearance. King played acoustic guitar and sang a solo of one of his favorite love songs, "Sea of Love." "I think we blew the doors off that place," King said.

In 1993, King suggested the writers reassemble for a five-city tour, ending at the American Book Association convention in Miami. They even had signed T-shirts made that proclaimed: "This band plays music as well as Metallica writes novels." In 1995, King was one of performers on a CD called *Stranger Than Fiction*. He played rhythm guitar and sang "Bo Diddley" and "Stand by Me". The CD featured some of America's top writing talents, with proceeds going to a fund that helps needy authors.

Still, King's writing remained far superior to his singing. In 1990, he published *Four Past Midnight*, a collection of short fiction. In 1991, *The Dark Tower III: The Wastelands* came out, first in a limited edition and later in mass form. *Needful Things* hit bookstores in that same year and was a main selection of the Book-of-the-Month Club.

Beginning in 1992, King published the first of what would become a trio of books exploring the abuse and exploitation of women. Although he had written about women before, most notably in *Carrie*, King's protagonists were typically male. Critic Chelsea Quinn Yarbro had written, "It is disheartening when a writer with so much talent and strength and vision is not able to develop a believable woman character between the ages of 17 and 60."

King agreed: most of his female characters were flat. Beginning with *Gerald's Game*, then, he began to write female protagonists. King wrote the story of Jessie, a woman who agrees to play a bondage game with her husband, who dies in the process, leaving her trapped in their isolated home. In his next female-heroine book, *Dolores Claiborne*, a mother and daughter deal with child sexual abuse, spousal abuse, and their relationships with men. The last in this trio of women-centered works, *Rose Madder*, also explores spousal abuse.

The 1990s saw a string of mediocre King movies and television miniseries. *Graveyard Shift*, *Sleepwalkers*, *The Dark Half*, and *Needful Things* all did well at theaters, and all were competent but by no means outstanding. On television, "The Tommyknockers," "Sometimes They Come Back," and "Stephen King's Golden Years" were unremarkable.

Beginning with *Misery* in 1990, though, a few King movies were truly exceptional. Years before, *Stand By Me* had proved that King's work could be made into great films, but until *Misery* no one had managed to do it since. *Misery* was funny, well-acted, and frightening. As maniacal fan Annie Wilkes, Kathy Bates earned a Golden Globe and an Academy Award. *The Shawshank Redemption* (1994) also rose far above the average; it was nominated for seven Academy Awards and won two Golden Globes. In that same year, the film version of *Dolores Claiborne*, also starring Kathy Bates, was released, to critical and commercial success. On television, the miniseries *The Stand* was better than most and King's remake of "The Shining" in 1997 captured a large audience and favorable reviews.

Through all this work and acclaim, King struggled to insulate his family and his soul from fame. Attention from fans and tourists who came to goggle at the Kings' unique house, as well as the constant phone calls requesting interviews and appearances from the media and others, had driven King to move the business side of his work to a nearby office building. The secretarial staff and manager worked out of this office, which King would visit in the afternoon to sign letters and review paperwork. He also used the office to conduct interviews, maintaining the privacy of his home. He kept his mornings free to write.

In April of 1992, one Erik Keene stopped in at the business office, asking for King's help in writing a book. He wanted King to house him for a few months, supply him with cigarettes and beer, and help him to write a novel. When the office staff didn't seem to think this was a workable idea, Keene became infuriated. King told his staff to call the police if Keene returned.

Two days later, he did. King and one of his sons were at a basketball game in Philadelphia, and Tabitha was home alone. Early in the morning, she heard glass breaking in the kitchen. She immediately went for the door, trying to get out, and she encountered Keene, who claimed to have a bomb. Tabitha, still in her pajamas, rushed to a neighbor's house and called the police. Sealing off the street, police used a canine unit to sniff out Keene. They found him in the attic with some cardboard and calculator parts put together to resemble a bomb.

Police discovered that Keene was a schizophrenic on parole in Texas. He pleaded not guilty to charges of burglary and not guilty by reason of insanity to charges terrorizing—and was convicted. But he promised to bring King a present "from the macabre", something his grandmother gave him before she died, if he ever got out. King immediately increased security at his home. "I don't want to live like Michael Jackson or like Elvis did at Graceland," King said. "That's gross. It was bad enough when we had to put up a fence. It was worse when we had to put up a gate. I hate to think I have to keep that gate locked."

Despite his reluctant efforts to protect his family's privacy, though, King always has been generous with his wealth and time. The Kings donated a hefty sum to help build a Massachusetts music, art, and theater center, naming the theater after King's mother. They funded half of the $1.5 million addition to the public library in Old Town, where Tabitha was raised. They also donated $1 million for a new baseball field after King, volunteering as assistant coach of Owen's Little League team, noticed that the fields were in poor shape. Nicknamed the Field of Screams, the state-of-the-art field was built behind his home in Bangor. The Kings also regularly contribute to the American Cancer Society and provide scholarships to local high school students.

EXPERIMENTS IN PUBLISHING

In the mid-1990s, following the episode with Keene, King turned his curiosity toward the publishing establishment. In the next few years he would come up with experiments in publishing that sent ripples through the industry.

In 1994, with the publication of *Insomnia*, the tale of an old man who loses his ability to sleep and awakens to a new look at his neighbors and family, King decided to go on tour again, something he hadn't done for years. But this wouldn't be the usual big-bookstore tour. King decided to visit only independent bookstores, traveling on his Harley Davidson motorcycle, decorated with a spider-web design. His efforts to promote the struggling independents made a splash in the press. King said he wanted to keep independent bookstores alive as a part of the downtown "scene" that makes a town unique. Besides, he said, "Borders doesn't need me."

His final stop was in Santa Cruz, California. Speaking at an auditorium on the final night of his tour, King condemned the chain stores for discounting books so much that small bookstores couldn't compete. Such focus on sales, he said, forces bookstores not to waste shelf space on authors who aren't going to sell a million copies. "It's not right," he said. "It's bad for diversity. It's bad for American thought when American fiction is represented only by Sidney Sheldon, Danielle Steele, Tom Clancy and Stephen King. That's not the way it's supposed to be, and it's a dangerous philosophy."

For his next experiment, King decided to feed his readers a novel piece by piece, knowing that some readers skip ahead to see how a story ends. The serial novel certainly wasn't new; in the 19th century, popular writers like Charles Dickens often published novels one installment at a time in the magazines of the day. But no one had tried it recently, and King believed that a serial novel would force his readers to read more or less in the way that he wanted, from beginning to ending.

The novel, *The Green Mile*, came out in 1996 in six installments, published at intervals of approximately one month. Fans loved the idea, and each slim volume sold a million copies. By August, when the last installment hit bookstores, King had six paperback bestsellers at one time. With King's next publishing experiment in that year, he would have eight simultaneous bestsellers, a record that has never been matched in the history of adult fiction.

King says publishing each section of *The Green Mile*—the story of a hulking black man with extraordinary healing powers who waits to die in a southern prison for two murders he didn't commit—before the completion of the novel invigorated his writing. As usual, King worked without an outline. He didn't know where the story would go. If he made a mistake and wrote a character into a corner, he could not rectify the situation easily. "I want to stay dangerous, and that means taking risks," he explained. "That is part of the excitement of the whole thing, though—at this point I'm driving through thick fog with the pedal all the way to the metal. It's like a novelistic striptease."

Two King novels released in 1996 had been conceived while he was driving Naomi's car back from Oregon in 1991. He had driven through the isolated town of Ruth, Nevada and wondered where all the people were. What if they were all dead? Who had killed them? His imagination answered: the local sheriff. Still considering the possibilities, King visited the town again during his independent bookstore tour to soak up the town's ambiance. He renamed the town Desperation and began work on a novel of the same name. The story begins much like King's visit when Johnny Marinville, a writer suffering a creative dry spell, rides his Harley into Desperation and finds things amiss.

After *Desperation*, King began *The Regulators*, based on an unpublished screenplay about a group of vigilante ghosts appearing in an unsuspecting western town to avenge a 100-year-old hanging. While writing, he heard the Voice:

> . . . [O]ne day I pulled up in my driveway after going to the market and the Voice said, "Do *The Regulators* and do it as a Bachman book and use the characters from *Desperation* but let them be who they're going to be in this story." Of course, the first thing I say when the Voice speaks up is "Bachman is dead," but the guy just laughs.

King obeyed and brought Bachman back from his 1986 death.

Writing as Bachman, King says, feels different. "When I put on my Bachman hat, I feel everyone just starts at 'Go' and there's no guarantee of a happy ending. It's tremendously liberating; Bachman doesn't have a conscience, he's not afraid to say things that I may be afraid to."

With two books about the same characters written by two different personas, King decided to do something unconventional. He would publish them as a "twinner" book: held in one orientation, the book would be *Desperation* by Stephen King; flipped over, it would be Bachman's *The Regulators*. When King approached his editors with the idea, they were reluctant but agreed , finding it hard to say no to Stephen King. With the publication of the twinner book, King had eight bestsellers at once.

While the general public devoured King's books in 1996, he worked on what his diehard fans wanted most—another *Dark Tower* book. Six years had passed since the previous installment, and letters from fans were becoming insistent.

It's always been my intention to finish. There isn't a day that goes by that I don't think about Roland and Eddie and Detta and all the other people, even Oy, the little animal. But this book has never done what I wanted it to do. I've been living with these guys longer than the readers have, ever since college, actually, and that's a long time ago for me.

In 1997, the fourth *Dark Tower* book, *Wizard & Glass*, came out, first in limited edition and then in mass publication. His fans were quieted, at least for a time. That same year, King's Philtrum Press published a limited edition of a collection, *Six Stories*.

That year he also made an innovative book deal for his novel *Bag of Bones*. Rather than take a large advance, like the $17 million he intended to ask for, King signed a deal that would give him a relatively small advance, but allow him a larger share of the profits. Typically, publishers only forward to writers only 10 to 20 percent of a book's sales; King's contract would give him 50 percent. The deal with Scribner, part of Simon & Schuster, meant King would see profits only when his work did. It is still too early to tell whether the arrangement will catch on in the publishing world, but if it does, then King's model will deserve credit for freeing publishers to take greater risks on unknown authors.

In 1999, three more King books hit the bookstores: *The Girl Who Loved Tom Gordon*, *Storm of the Century*, and *Hearts in Atlantis*; but in the middle of the year King's life took an unexpected turn. On June 19, he walked his daily four-mile trek near his summer home, reading as usual. All his children and his first grandchild, just three months old, were visiting. As he approached a hill where the shoulder narrowed, King lowered the book to watch for traffic.

Bryan Smith, a 42-year-old former construction worker, was driving his blue Dodge Caravan when his dog started nosing around in his cooler. Smith turned to push the dog away. The van swerved and, at 45 miles per hour, hit King with so much force that King's head shattered the windshield and he was hurled over the van, landing in a ditch some 14 feet away. "I'm lying in the ditch and there's blood all over my face and my right leg hurts," King remembered. "I look down and see something I don't like: my lap now appears to be on sideways, as if my whole lower body had been wrenched half a turn to the right."

An ambulance rushed King to a nearby hospital. He had severe injuries—a shattered hip and pelvis, four broken ribs, a punctured lung, a fractured thighbone, scalp lacerations that would require 20 or 30 stitches, eight spine chips, a split right knee, and a left knee pulverized into marble-sized pieces. He was taken by helicopter to a trauma center in Lewiston.

During the flight his lung collapsed, and paramedics inserted a chest tube. He listened to the strange sound of his breath through the tube. King later recalled his thoughts:

> I don't want to die. I love my wife, my kids, my afternoon walks by the lake. I also love to write; I have a book on writing that's sitting back home on my desk, half-finished. I don't want to die, and as I lie in the helicopter looking out at the bright blue summer sky, I realized that I'm actually lying in death's doorway. Someone is going to pull me one way or the other pretty soon; it's mostly out of my hands.

During the next three weeks, King underwent six surgeries. When he returned home in July, the pain was excruciating and he could barely sit up. He had a hospital bed set up in the sunroom on the ground floor and spent the next few weeks playing with his dog, Marlowe, and his guitar. He dreaded the long, intense rehabilitation. He wondered whether his desire or ability to write had been shattered along with his body; he said to a Dateline reporter, shortly after returning home, "Maybe there'll be another book. Maybe there won't."

Near the end of July, he decided to try. Tabitha set up a desk, a computer, and reference books at the end of the hall.

She got me positioned at the table, kissed me on the temple, and then left me there to find out if I had anything left to say. It turned out I did, a little, but without her intuitive understanding that yes, it was time, I'm not sure either of us would ever have found that out for sure.

That first writing session lasted an hour and forty minutes. . . . When it was over, I was dripping with sweat and almost too exhausted to sit up straight in my wheelchair . . . And the first 500 words were uniquely terrifying—it was as if I'd never written anything before them in my life.

By October, King could move around well enough on crutches to see his beloved Red Sox play at Fenway Park in Boston and visit his son Joe and grandson Ethan. In December, King managed to make it to New York for the premiere of the film version of *The Green Mile*.

Smith, King discovered, had been charged with 11 violations in as many years for speeding and driving while intoxicated. Smith pleaded not guilty to aggravated assault, and through plea bargaining his sentence was reduced to six months, suspended, and a one-year suspension of his license. King believed with his history of poor driving, Smith's license should have been taken permanently. He called the lenient sentence "irresponsible public business."

The family spent most of that winter in Florida, where King wouldn't have to worry about falling on the ice and could spend time with Naomi, then 29. His desire to write returned, as strong as before. He finished a novella, some short stories, and a non-fiction book, *On Writing*, and he began with Peter Straub the collaboration that would become *Black House*.

With the new millennium, King undertook another publishing experiment. This time he bypassed bookstores and publishers altogether. King had been using the Internet for several years, with Web sites for his books and movies getting plenty of visitors. Indeed, King may well be at the forefront of a revolution in publishing. Industry experts say that within two decades, 90 percent of books will be released not in paper but online—as e-books, either documents structured for downloading or online consumption or CDs that are easily portable and can carry dozens of novels each.

King began the electronic development of his work early. While the Internet was growing, the idea of the e-book took hold. Publishers and authors saw that the Web might eventually be a market for readers. Thousands of works were already being offered as downloads in 2000, but it was only when King tried it in that same year that readers took notice. In March, King put his short story "Riding the Bullet" online, and within days the burden of half a million attempts to download the story crashed the site.

A few months later, King tried Internet publishing again—this time with a novel. King released *The Plant* in 5,000-word segments. For each download, a person was asked to send $1 by mail; part of the experiment was to see how many people would send in the money. King promised to publish at least two segments. Whether he published the rest depended on whether people actually sent in the payments. His rule was that if 75 percent of the people paid for the installments, he would keep providing them. But less than half of the people who downloaded it sent in their payments and, true to his word, King ended the project.

Just before the accident, in the spring of 1999, King and Tabitha were driving back from Florida and had stopped at a little gas station when, as King walked behind the building in search of a bathroom, accident led to inspiration. There was a stream at the bottom of a slope that was layered with melting snow; King slipped, grabbing a cast-out engine block just in time to save himself from sliding into the water. The experience, in a manner typical of King's creativity, would engender a new work:

> I found myself wondering, had that happened, how long it would have taken the gas station attendant to call the state police if my car, a brand-new Lincoln Navigator, just continued to stand there in front of the pumps. By the time I got back on the turnpike again, I had two things: a wet ass from my fall behind the Mobil station, and a great idea for a story."

AIMEE LABRIE

Stephen King: Exorcising the Demons

The genre or horror fiction has long been a subject of both criticism and fascination. While writers such as Edgar Allan Poe, Mary Shelley, and Bram Stoker have been accepted into the literary canon (some more readily or thoroughly than others), contemporary horror writers have had more difficulty in gaining access. Peter Straub, Dean Koontz, and Anne Rice have made their names and fortunes producing novels that sell almost as soon as they are shelved, but they are not considered artists whose work will endure beyond their lifetime. Similarly, Stephen King, America's most popular and prolific horror writer, is largely dismissed by academics as a writer of pulp fiction, useful in providing beach reading or mindless entertainment, but not someone whose craft should be taken seriously.

This belief is born in part of the prolific nature of King's writing. To date, he has published more than thirty-three novels, four short story collections, and three e-books and has written six screenplays for movies or television—and he is currently working on nineteen new projects, including movie contracts for his books *Bag of Bones*, *Eyes of the Dragon*, *The Girl Who Loved Tom Gordon*, *The Sun Dog*, *Desperation*, and *The Mist*. Two books will see publication in 2002: *Everything's Eventual* and *From a Buick Eight*. All his books have become bestsellers.

The question interviewers ask King most frequently is why he writes horror. How could a writer of King's background create the dreamed rape of a bound girl in "Apt Pupil" (from *Different Seasons*)? Or the ending of the 1982 short story "The Raft": a doctor, stranded, eating himself incrementally with a scalpel? King explains his attraction to the horrific in Tim Underwood and Chuck Miller's *Bare Bones: Conversations on Terror with Stephen King*:

> . . . it's a kind of psychological protection. It's like drawing a magic circle around my family and myself. My mother always used to say, "If you think the worst, it can't come true." I know that's superstition, but I've always believed that if you think the very worst, then, no matter how bad things get (and in my heart I've always been convinced that they can get pretty bad), they'll never get as bad as *that*. If you write a novel where the boogeyman gets somebody else's children, maybe they'll never get your own children. . . . For me, writing is like a little hole in reality that you can go through and you can get out and you can be someplace else for a while. I live a very ordinary life. I have the children, and I have the wife—except for this thing I do, this glitch, it's a very ordinary life. (3–4)

Aside from its providing a psychological release, King believes that reading and watching horror serves as "a rehearsal for death". "It's a way to get ready," he says in *Bare Bones*. "People say there's nothing sure but death and taxes. But that's not really true. There's really only death, you know. Death is the biggie. Two hundred years from now, none of us are going to be here." (10) In his introduction to the short story collection *Night Shift*, he further explains the impetus for his writing:

> The sludge that catches in the mesh of my drain is often the stuff of fear. My obsession is with the macabre . . . I am not a great artist, but I have always felt impelled to write. So each day I sift the sludge anew, going through the cast-off bits and pieces of observation, of memory, of speculation, trying to make something out of the stuff that didn't go through the filter and down the drain into the subconscious. (635)

King's life might be compared to that of a character in Dickens. He was born on in Portland, Maine, in 1947, to Donald and Nellie Ruth King. When he was two years old, his father, ostensibly going out for a pack of cigarettes, disappeared; King never heard from him again. King's mother struggled to support her family, working as a baker and a laundress. He and his older brother David spent much of their time alone and wore clothing handed down from their neighbors and friends. King's childhood contained elements of fear and suspense. His earliest memory is of dropping a cinderblock on his foot and then being attacked by wasps from the nest underneath—a scene that would later appear near the beginning of *The Shining*. He remembers being evicted from the family home in West DePere, Wisconsin after someone saw his six-year-old brother crawling on the roof. And because his mother worked so much, he and his brother were often watched by incompetent babysitters. One example goes beyond incompetence and almost into sadism: a sixteen-year old African-American girl named Beulah once made King eat seven fried eggs and then locked him into a closet, where his mother later discovered him asleep with egg-vomit dried into his hair. (21)

Because he was prone to infections of the ear and throat, King spent much of his time as a child reading comic books and Jack London tales and eventually began copying them. His mother, after reading his first story and finding he copied most of it, advised him to "'Write one of your own, Stevie,' she said. 'Those *Combat Casey* books are just junk . . . I bet you could do better. Write one of your own.'" King's next story was an original one, something about four magical animals in a car. His mother awarded him a quarter. What he remembers most about this experience is "an immense feeling of *possibility* at the idea, as if I had been ushered into a vast building filled with closed doors and had been given leave to open any I liked. There were more doors than one person could ever open in a lifetime, I thought (and still think)." [*On Writing*, 28]

From then on, King continued to write. He sold his first "book" on the playground at the age of seven, a serial comic book that owed much to Poe's *The Pit and the Pendulum*. He was caught by school officials and made to give the money back to his classmates. Still, the experience taught him that he could create something that other people would like. It was while working in the attic of his house in Durham on a royal-blue Underwriter with missing keys—as keys would later be missing from Annie's typewriter in *Misery*—that he saw his first rejection ("Happy Stamps", *Alfred Hitchcock's Mystery Magazine*) and his first publication ("In a Half-World of Terror" in a horror fanzine). His first paycheck came, in his seventeenth year, from *Fantasy and Science Fiction* for "The Night of the Tiger". It would be only a few years later, when King was in his early twenties, that Doubleday would purchase *Carrie* for $400,000; but King developed early in his career the idea that the writing was what counted.

When King was seven, he discovered a dusty box of paperbacks in the attic garage above his aunt's house. With the exception of an old reel of film on which his father appears momentarily, these books were the only relics of the missing man. These included cheaply printed horror books from Avon, issues of *Weird Tales*, H.P. Lovecraft's short stories, and discarded manuscripts of stories his father had tried to write. This first encounter with pulp fiction led King to the lurid E.C. comic books and William M. Gaine's horror comics *Tales from the Crypt*, *The Haunts of Fear*, and *The Vault of Horror*—stories that focused largely on supernatural revenge. As he grew older, he sought out more serious works like *Dracula*, *Burnt Offerings* and *Frankenstein*, along with the works of H.P. Lovecraft, Ray Bradbury, and Harlan Ellison. He continued to write, and he continued to model his work after the plotlines he most enjoyed. Examples of this style are found in the structure of the vampire novel *Salem's Lot*, a contemporary rewriting of Bram Stoker's *Dracula*, and in the setting of *The Shining*, which is reminiscent of Shirley Jackson's *The Haunting of Hill House* and also of Poe's "The Masque of the Red Death." *Pet Sematary*, the story of a man who can bring back the dead by burying them in an Indian burial ground, contains elements of Mary Shelley's *Frankenstein*, and the resurrection of Louis Creed's wife bears a resemblance to W.W. Jacob's "The Monkey's Paw". King seems well aware of his tendency to reframe his writing from the things he loves. In his non-fiction book *On Writing*, King addresses this act of mimicry: "This sort of stylistic blending is a necessary part of the development of one's own style." [147]

He acknowledges the influences of cinematic horror as well. The first film he remembers with any clarity is one he saw at a drive-in theater at the age of seven. Although he knew *The Creature from the Black Lagoon* was purely fictional and mostly ridiculous, in *Danse* Macabre he recalls being terrified: "My reaction to the creature on that night was perhaps the perfect reaction, the one every writer of horror fiction . . . hopes for when he or she uncaps a pen: total emotional involvement, pretty much undiluted by an real thinking process. . . ." [99] From there, he became a bona fide horror fan, and he lists *The Texas Chainsaw Massacre*, *Invasion of the Body Snatchers*, *The Omen*, *The Exorcist*, and *Freaks* as some of his favorites. He references these films directly in elements like the dead woman in the shower in *The Shining* (Hitchcock's infamous shower scene in *Psycho*) and the living-stalking corpses of *Pet Sematary* (the zombies in *The Night of the Living Dead*). *The Tommyknockers*, *Desperation*, and *The Regulators*, among numerous short stories, are more science fiction than horror. They contain the seeds of the B-movies King loved as a child, such as *Them*, *The Day the Earth Stood Still*, and *Earth vs. the Flying Saucers*.

It may be also said that King's interest in horror films is part of what developed the staccato images he constructs by inter-splicing scenes and using short, simple sentences. Particularly in scenes of violence, his paragraphs read like snapshots. In part, this style may be helpful to heighten climactic moments using visual details rather than interior monologue or narration:

He brought the mallet down again and this time she rolled toward him, down the stairs, inside the arc of his swing. A shriek escaped her as her broken ribs thumped and grated. She struck his shins with her body while he was off balance and he backed with a yell of anger and surprise, his feet jiggling to keep their purchase on the stair rise. Then he thumped to the floor, the mallet flying from his hand. He sat up, starting at her for a moment with shocked eyes. [*The Shining*, 283]

Halfway through his second spin, Steve let her go. Audrey flew backward like a stone cast out of a sling, her feet stuttering on the floor, still caterwauling. Cynthia, who was behind her, dropped to her hands and knees with the speed of a born playground survivor. Audrey collided with her shin-high and went over backward, sprawling on the lighter-colored rectangle where the second projects had rested. She stared up at them through the tumble of her hair, momentarily dazed. [*Desperation*, 478]

"What are you taking about?" Brad asks. He's lying full-length on his stomach. Now he takes the figure, which is perhaps seven inches tall, from Johnny and looks at it. There is a cut on one of Brad's plump cheeks. Falling glass from the light-fixture, Johnny assumes. Downstairs, the screaming woman falls silent. Brad looks at the alien, then stares at Johnny with eyes that are almost comically round. "You're full of shit," he says. [*The Regulators*, 194]

This stylistic choice again pays homage to the cinematic images that have enthralled him since *The Creature from the Black Lagoon*. By writing scenes that read like script directions, King constructs a visual narrative that allows him not only to juggle several characters at once, but also to heighten the suspense. Although this stylistic model appears early in his work, he has continued to follow it in part because of his success in the crossover to films.

Another quality of King's writing is his grounding of most of his works in the New England landscape, particularly in Maine. He does set some in other states—California, Nebraska, and Nevada, for instance—but, for the most part, they are in the East, near places where King where he was raised and now lives. Instead of referring to a real town, King has invented his own places: Jerusalem, Castle Rock, and Desperation. These creations retain the geography and qualities of real towns like Bangor, Maine, but they also allow him to maintain his blending of fact and fiction

King's novels are considered "page-turners"—the kind of book that keeps readers moving through the story to find out how it all ends, whether they see larger symbolism in the tale or not. While his story lines are often fantastical, King strives to make the human reactions of the characters recognizable. A child with destructive telekinesis; a mother and son terrorized by a rabid dog; a writer trapped in a home of a maniac-depressive serial killer with an aversion to harsh language; or a neighborhood taken over by the characters from a children's show—King allows his stories to strain credibility. "But within the framework of the stories," he adds in *Feast of Fear*, "I'm concerned that what the people do in these stories should be as real as possible and the characters should be real people." [232] He invites readers to relax into a world they recognize, only then to introduce the monster— the implication being that what befalls the character might easily befall the reader. King realizes that "book buyers want a good story . . . This happens, I think, when readers recognize the people in a book, their behaviors, their surroundings and their talk. When the reader hears a strong echo of his or her life and beliefs, he or she is apt to become more invested in the story." [*On Writing*, 161]

King even gives the supernatural credit for the source of his stories. To keep the story suspenseful, King claims that he tunes into the "basement man" rather than outlining an intricate plotline ahead of time. This is a difficult point for him to carry; the modern belief usually is that writing is a craft and that it takes courage, time, stamina, and a fair amount of egotism. King, then, either is driven by something in the writing or keeps thirty little Stephen Kings locked in that "basement". He sees writing more as a kind of possession by the story than as a mastery of the story: "If I'm not able to guess with any accuracy how the damned thing is going to turn out even with my inside knowledge of events, I can be pretty sure of keeping the reader in a state of page-turning anxiety." [*On Writing*, 165] The motto of the men's club in his story "The Breathing Method" confirms his belief that what's important: "It is the tale, not he who tells it."

King frequently references brand names and elements of popular culture. He eliminates abstractions; he deals with the concrete. His novels and short stories are filled with *things*, not just monsters and frights. One could create a pastiche of consumer culture from them: *Scooby Doo*, Virginia Slims, Jim Beam, Budweiser, *Perry Mason*, Lysol, Mickey Mouse, Rolex, Banana Republic, *One Life to Live*, Toyota, Baby Ruth, Slurpies, Ryder trucks, Duracell batteries. King also writes about the less commonly mentioned aspects of human life: shitting, farting, pants-wetting, nose-picking. His pejoratives, which he wields as freely as he does adjectives, form a list far too extensive to go into here. Essays might be written about his scatological references: "Shit-fire and save matches!" in *The Regulators* [452] or "Hargensen called up after school . . . and asked her if she knew pig poop was spelled C-A-R-R-I-E" in *Carrie* [875]. King uses this device and similar devices to portray his characters' expression more believably, despite the objections of purists: "Look out for the Legion of Decency. They might not like the word *shit* and you might not like it much, either, but sometimes you're just stuck with it—no kid ever went to his mother and said that his little sister just *defecated* in the bathtub." [*On Writing*, 186]

Along these same lines, King's characters, both good and bad, are ordinary people, of the middle or lower classes. They drive battered cars and live in tract homes in the suburbs. The kids ride scooters, play with action figures, and want night-lights to keep away the monsters. These are regular folk, often on the social periphery, who find themselves in desperate situations. Many of King's characters might be called "losers", too—such as Carrie White (*Carrie*) and Arnie Cunningham (*Christine*), whose social awkwardness, and its resultant isolation, has deadly consequences. King's "losers" inevitably must make choices either to turn to rage, and become an force of evil, or to integrate into social groups through selfless acts and side with the "good guys". Johnny Marinville, the motorcycling protagonist of *Desperation*, runs away from his failure as a writer. When he comes up against a supernatural spirit called Tak, he is forced to decide whether he's going to follow his own interest and flee the town or stay with the others to help to defeat the demon. He chooses the latter, finally sacrificing his life to save the group. Interestingly, his dying words are, "God forgive me, I hate critics!"[*Desperation*, 668]

King's books in general cover similar themes and patterns, but as he matures as a writer these are honed and expanded. Like a spiral staircase, they move around the same subject matter with a sense of circular ascension. Surely the themes in his books and short stories work in many ways to circle King's fears, whether in a particular role (as a father, a teacher, or a writer) or in alleviating his personal terrors. A list of these is given in Hoppenstand Browne's *The Gothic World of Stephen King*: fears of snakes, squishy things, deformity, rats, enclosed spaces, insects (especially spiders, flies, beetles), death, and others (paranoia)—and fear *for* someone else. [11]

Although not all of King's fears can be pinpointed directly in his writing, patterns can be found that suggest his fears are the impetus for much of his writing. First of all, families are fragmented and dysfunctional. Marriages fail, partners commit adultery, and parents are not to be trusted. Tony Magistrale points out in *Landscape of Fear* that in King's world "[the adults'] behavior is often immature and without consequence" and that "their institutions—the church, the state's massive bureaucratic system of control,

the nuclear family itself—barely mask an undercurrent of violence." [77]
Instead of being the all-American baseball-throwing dads—as King himself
is, in many ways, on the surface—the men are capable of murder. Jack
Torrance, the father in *The Shining*, takes a winter job as caretaker of the
haunted Overlook Hotel after struggles with alcoholism and, more recently,
the abuse of his young son. Pressured by the supernatural in the hotel,
Torrance hallucinates and becomes homicidal, ultimately chasing his wife
and son with an axe. "The Boogeyman" traces another father's descent into
madness, incrementally giving the reader to understand that the Boogeyman
in his son's closet is not an imagined threat but a very real one. The mother
figures in King's work are no less misshapen. Carrie White's fanatical mother
meets her daughter at the door and attacks her with a butcher knife to save
her from sin. Donna Trenton in *Cujo* manages to entrap herself and her son
in a car while a rabid dog menaces outside. In short, the characters in King's
novels would do better to flee from home than to run toward it. Perhaps
because part of King's goal as a writer is to offer a reflection of his culture,
these heightened situations involve grotesque distortions of the American
family.

King writes fiction that reflects his own life in very similar ways,
although, of course, the situations are exaggerated. As one of the world's
most recognizable novelists, King has wrestled the problems accompanying
his fame. He lives with his family in a Victorian house surrounded by a large
wrought-iron fence spiked with gargoyles. He has had his share of stalkers.
It is not surprising than that many of his male characters are writers
struggling with the difficulties that accompany the job. *The Dark Half*, for
example, centers on writer Thad Beaumont, who has constructed a persona
named George Stark to pen a series of crime novels. Beaumont decides that
he would like to try his hand at more literary work, but his other self comes
to life to stop him. In *Misery*, novelist Paul Sheldon wants to retire his most
popular character, the perpetually sweet and perpetually suffering Misery
Chastain. After a life-threatening accident, Sheldon finds himself bed-ridden
in the isolated farmhouse of serial killer and self-proclaimed "number one
fan" Annie Wilkes and forced to write what his reader desires him to write—
and Wilkes even destroys his just-finished attempt at another genre. In both
novels, the protagonist struggles to be taken seriously as a writer. King, too,
has published under a pseudonym in order to release more than one book per
year without saturating the market. As Richard Bachman, he has published
six books, the last of which (*The Regulators*) was supposed to come from
Bachman after his death from cancer. In the preface to *Four Past Midnight*'s
"Secret Window, Secret Garden" (1990), King assures the reader that "this
story is, I think, the last story about writers and writing and the strange no

man's land which exists between what's real and what's make believe." [239] Not true; in *Bag of Bones* (1990), thriller writer Mike Noonan finds that every time he sits down at the computer to work he vomits.

King has always found fascination in writing about children. In *Reading Stephen King*, he explains that

> . . . you cannot be an adult in this or any society until you have finished with your childhood and one must commonly does this by raising children of one's own. But there is nothing thematic about the way [*Different* Seasons] feels to me; like "The Body," it is about what I remember . . . in my own childhood: love and terror and finding a hand to hold when things get hard and living in the world hurts. [17]

In his early works, these children have extraordinary powers. Charlie McKee in *Firestarter* is gifted with pyrokinesis, the ability to cause combustion at will. Because of this talent, Charlie is pursued by "the Shop," a faceless group of government officials who want to use Charlie as a kind of terrorist weapon against other countries. Danny Torrance of *The Shining* has what's called "the Shine," a kind of clairvoyance. Twelve-year-old Jack Sawyer of *The Talisman*, co-written with Peter Straub, can flip the present world into an alternate universe he calls "the Territories." By moving between the Territories and his own universe, he succeeds in saving the Queen, his mother's double. *Desperation*'s young protagonist uses a direct line to God and to stay ahead of evil forces. *The Regulators* features an autistic boy who again is able to channel the evildoer's intentions—although he is himself possessed by the monster much of the time.

Other young characters start out as innocents who end up crossing over into adulthood. "The Body" from *Different Seasons* catalogues the trek of four boys to see the corpse of a fifth who has been run over by a train. This may be among the most overtly autobiographical of King's pieces.

When the children in King's stories are corrupt, this change occurs unnaturally, most often because of a parental figure or lack thereof. "Apt Pupil" from *Different Seasons* centers on the gradual corruption of Todd Bowden, a twelve-year-old Californian who discovers that his neighbor is a former officer of a Nazi death camp. Bowden, fascinated by the horror of the Holocaust, asks the commander, Kurt Dussander, to tell him stories, proclaiming that "I want to hear about it . . . Everything. All of the gooshy stuff." [*Different Seasons* 124] The story ends with a transformed Bowden waiting on freeway with a rifle poised to shoot. "Children of the Corn" is a story about the teenage inhabitants of a small Nebraska town who have taken the fantastical religion of their parents to an extreme, murdering them and offering up human sacrifices to their corn god.

Pet Sematary might be King's most disturbing book. In an interview with *Playboy*, he explained that he wrote it first in response to his daughter Naomi's fear that her cat would be killed. But in *Landscape of Fear*, Magistrale refers to the 1984 International Conference of Fantastical Artists, at which King gave a lecture and then fielded questions: "Someone in the audience asked Stephen King the question 'What terrifies you the most?' King's reply was emphatic and immediate: 'Opening the door of my children's bedroom and finding on of them dead.'" [73] In the book, three-year-old Gage is struck by a truck and killed. In his overwhelming grief, Gage's father returns his son's corpse to the sacred Micmac Indian burial grounds, even though he knows Gage will return not as the boy he knows but as a demonic force. After he finished the book, King put it away in a drawer for two years, and he claims not to have read it since.

Over the years, King has continued to focus on the influence of children on the adult world. Yet his use of children as central characters has diminished, a change that he says has occurred because his children have grown and he wants to move on to different themes, perhaps exploring his adult characters in greater depth. Children are still present (most notably in *Desperation* and *The Regulators*), but mainly as sidekicks or victims who need to be rescued by the central male figures. In his later works, childhood becomes a point of historical reference for the current action rather than the action itself. In *It*, "The Body", *Cujo*, and *The Shining*, the main action of the tale occurs in childhood. In *Dreamcatcher* and *Black House*, children present information, but both works focus on the adult male. *Black House* most clearly illustrates this process as it deals with the adult life of Jack Sawyer, who was 12 years old in *The Talisman*.

The motivation behind some unfavorable criticism of King's writing is easy to divine. First, he writes horror fiction, a genre that throughout its development has generally been considered lowbrow. Also, he is perhaps the nation's, or the world's, most popular living writer, and he is the only writer ever to see all his or her books on the bestseller list. Because of this popularity and subject matter, King's work seems by some to be a product to be consumed by the masses rather than a work of literary merit. He falls in line with other writers whose work is not considered substantive: John Grisham, Sue Grafton, Danielle Steele. The authorial company he keeps and his appeal to a mass audience suggest that his work is intended to be read quickly and discarded.

King has also been criticized for creating flat female characters that never evolve beyond the stock role of wife or mother. Wendy Torrance from

The Shining is probably less intelligent than the St. Bernard in *Cujo*, which also trumps her in efficacy. Having managed at last to trap her crazed husband in the hotel's freezer, she still ponders whether she should unlock the door. She does. *Desperation*'s mother—"Mrs. Suburban Wifemom, on her way to a nice middle-class vacation in Lake Tahoe, where she had probably planned to wear her new resort clothes from Talbot's over her new underwear from Victoria's Secret" [468]—ends up being kidnapped and possessed by an evil spirit, in which form she tries to find and murder her son. Annie Wilkes is a serial killer whose mania takes the undeveloped form of perverted motherhood. Nadine of *The Stand* is a succubus. Even in the recent *Black House*, the primary female characters either are insane or soon will be and must be rescued by the heroic male Jack Sawyer. Additionally, one of the most common reflexes of women in his stories is to burst into tears.

King has had an awareness of this dysfunction as early as the construction of Carrie White, when he almost stopped writing the book because he lost interest in the character and felt inept at constructing an authentic female protagonist. In *Salem's Lot*, for example, Susan Norton becomes a vampire who stalks her boyfriend (and not very well—he is able to kill her almost instantly). In recent years, he has attempted to center stories on female characters, as in *Gerald's Game* (1992) and *Rose Madder* (1995), both novels that attempt to deal with women caught in abusive situations. But the women in these books don't move beyond their victimization. *Dolores Claiborne* (1993), a story about two women searching for escape from their abusive husbands, is a more successful in this respect, and the women fight back against their husbands: Vera cuts the brakes on her husband's BMW, and Dolores tricks her husband into falling down a well. Still, both women are defined by and reduced to their positions as wives, Dolores is guilty of marrying a man capable of incest and Vera of staying in a marriage for wealth, and both achieve liberation only through murder.

Similarly, his African-American characters, while they may have grown in complexity—moving from the spiritual guides of Halloran in *the Shining* to Mother Abigail in *The Stand* to less marginalized roles in *It*, *The Regulators*, and *The Green Mile*—do not appear to do much more than assist or guide the almost exclusively white-male protagonists. King's successful *The Green Mile* (1996) is narrated by prison guard Paul Edgecombe, who details his experiences with Jon Coffey, an African-American inmate on death row. Coffey's parallels to Jesus Christ are readily apparent: he has the power to heal; he is sacrificed and raised from the dead. Essentially, though, Coffey is a throwback to notions of the mysterious/primal/"native" black man. Coffey remains unaware of his powers, devolving from a healer to a man incapable of tying his shoes, defending himself, or remembering whether he has dined.

The story is not about him as much as it is about what he can teach the white man. After Coffey heals his urinary tract infection, Edgecombe supposes, "[A]s for Coffey himself, he had probably already forgotten about it. He was nothing but a conduit, after all, and there isn't a culvert in the world that remembers the water that flowed through it once the rain has stopped." [192] Of course, it is not necessarily the writer's job to take up the cause for every group who has suffered discrimination. Still, while one can see an attempt on King's part to work out his difficulties in filling out his female and black characters, he has yet to write his way out of his typical representation.

Another common criticism of King's work is that he does not take the craft of writing seriously enough. In *Danse Macabre*, for example, he claims to have written *The Stand*—a work of 1,138 pages—in part for the joy of nihilism: "No more Ronald McDonald! No more Gong Show or *Soap* on TV—just soothing snow. No more terrorists! No more bullshit! . . . I got a chance to scrub the whole human race. And it was *fun!*" [373] Though the length of his work does vary—he had to insert news clippings and letters into *Carrie* for the book to be considered a novel—his more recent books, such as *Desperation*, *Hearts in Atlantis*, *Dreamcatcher*, and *Black House* (with Peter Straub) are of the same girth as *The Stand*. Given the sheer volume of his books in tandem with the rapidity of their production, critics have difficulty in believing that King spends much time on his craft, though he claims to write 10,000 words a day, every day. In addition, his books vacillate, some hailed as great writing and others as better doorstop than fiction. King admits he writes quickly, usually finishing a draft in a few months and rewriting it only once or twice. Additionally, though he has been sober for over twelve years, he acknowledges that he barely remembers writing *Cujo* or *The Shining* and that he wrote *The Running Man* in two weeks. One could argue that it is discipline that enables him to produce volumes of work; the larger issue is of whether this work is of any merit.

Whether one is a fan of King or not, it does seem that his personal and writing life could be scripted from one of his own stories. It is "Local Boy Makes Good" with this twist: years after making good, Local Boy loses the ability to do the thing he loves most when he is crippled while walking along the side of the highway. On June 19, 1999, King was taking his daily walk when he was hit by a van riding on the shoulder of the road. His leg was broken in seven places, and his recuperation took several months. In an essay entitled "On Impact" that originally appeared in *The New Yorker* and was later anthologized in *The Best American Essays: 2001*, King writes:

> I didn't want to go back to work. I was in a lot of pain, unable to
> bend my right knee . . . Yet, at the same time, I felt that I was all

out of choices. I had been in terrible situations before and writing had helped me get over them—had helped me to forget myself, at least for a little while.

On some days, that writing is a pretty grim slog. On others—more and more of them, as my mind reaccustoms itself to its old routine—I feel that buzz of happiness, that sense of having found the write words and put them in line. It's like lifting off in an airplane: you're on the ground, on the ground, on the ground, on the ground . . . and then you're up, riding on a cushion of air and the prince of all you survey. (128–129, 130–131)

It does seem that the act of writing has been and continues to be King's sustenance.

MICHAEL R. COLLINGS

King and the Critics

To talk about King and critics is tremendously difficult, if only because of the enormous range of statements made about King by critics and about critics by King—to say nothing of King's own contributions to social, cultural, and literary criticism. Each perspective on King results in different possibilities; each works under different (and often mutually exclusive) presuppositions about art and literature; and each addresses radically differing audiences. In this chapter, I have divided an otherwise impossibly cumbersome topic into several more manageable subtopics, beginning with the most accessible and vocal forms of criticism—popular criticism as epitomized by reviews, review-articles, and interviews in daily, weekly, and monthly publications as diverse as the *New York Times Book Review*, the *Kirkus Review*, and *The Orange Country Register*.

1. Popular Mainstream Criticism

In *The Valley Advocate* for 21 July 1986, Stanley Wiater borrowed the title of this study for an article examining the extent of King's influence and of the increasing critical interest in King.

Wiater outlines the three most important recent directions in King scholarship and criticism: Underwood-Miller's collections of essays, *Fear*

From *The Stephen King Phenomenon*. © 1985 Starmont House. Reprinted with permission.

Itself: The Horror Fiction of Stephen King, Kingdom of Fear: The World of Stephen King, and a third volume currently in preparation; Douglas E. Winter's 1982 *Stephen King* (which he refers to as *The Reader's Guide to Stephen King*) and its subsequent enlargement as *Stephen King: The Art of Darkness* (1984; 1986); and the Starmont series, *which* he notes is "on a somewhat more 'scholarly' level" than the others. Ostensibly an overview of criticism, Wiater's article serves equally well as an introduction to the difficulty of working with (and writing) King criticism. The article seems oddly schizophrenic, at once inviting and mildly disapproving of such endeavors. While acknowledging that King is a cultural phenomenon, Wiater refers sarcastically to the increasing intensity of critical study: "Yet for the millions of devoted readers who won't leave home without him [King], comes some erudite relief—even more books, not written by King, but about the man and his work." Such books may well become the "next cottage industry in the publishing world," he continues, as they "dissect every corner of the 'Stephen King Phenomenon.'"

Wiater even includes a brief quotation from King relevant to this critical attention. In a tone somewhat moderated from his earlier statements about critics (in the *Adelina* reviews, for example), King defers judgment:

> It's a little bit like Huck Finn and Tom Sawyer going to their own funeral. I'm aware of them. I've read them. For example, Collings' book, *The Many Facets of Stephen King*, which is the latest volume in this parade; has a marvelous and insightful essay on *The Eyes of the Dragon*, which is the children's book that I wrote that will be out in a year or two. That's a good piece. But beyond that, what can I say? They're there, and some of them are good, and some of them are bad, and I'm not going to pick them apart. It's not my place.

Criticism, King concludes, is "their business, not mine. I just write stories." The article is symptomatic of a difficulty that has followed King's writing from the beginning. At first it was difficult to find neutral—to say nothing of favorable—criticism of King's novels; now, when critics have begun to take him seriously and to explore the complexities of the worlds he creates, they are themselves not taken quite seriously; the prevailing attitude seems to be that there must be something self-serving in someone who devotes this much time and effort to a writer who is himself "academically" suspect.

As a writer, of course, King has confronted this attitude innumerable times; in an interview with Loukia Louka for the *Maryland Coast Dispatch* (8

August 1986), when asked how he responds to attacks that he is "not very literary," King answered:

> I don't spend a lot of time worrying about it. If people ask me if I will ever do anything serious, my response is that I'm serious every time I sit down to write. You decide whether or not what I've done is serious. I try as hard as I can. It is not really for me to say or judge what I do. I do the best I can and the rest of it is up to the critics. Much of it will be decided 50 years after I'm dead. Either the stuff will still be knocking around or it won't. I think some of it will be. It might not be taught in upper level English classes. I'm not sure that is its place. But I think it will be there. Kids will still be checking 'Salem's Lot out of the library. Horror stories have an incredible staying power" (86).

The comment is apt and appropriate; on the other side of the coin, however, King is not entirely satisfied with commonplace judgments about himself and his writing. Stephen Beeber asked what King thought about the fact that for the past decade every novel he has published became a best seller. King replied:

> It upsets me in a way sometimes. By being a bestseller I get the feeling that there's just some kind of composite of the average American sitting between my ears, that I fall into the midground of literature—I guess I'd like to think I'm a little better than that. (16–A)

Perhaps he is; but he is undoubtedly in a difficult situation as far as critical reactions go. Since he has chalked up such remarkable commercial successes, it has become almost an article of faith among mainstream critics that he is not a writer worth talking about.

During late July and early August, 1986, a number of articles appeared that discussed two films: *Maximum Overdrive* written and directed by King; and *Stand by Me*, based on "The Body," a novella from *Different Seasons*. The reactions to the films aptly define the current state of criticism.

Associating King's name with a film almost automatically endangers the project. Susin Shapiro focuses on this problem in her "One Picture is Worth a Million Words." "No matter what I do," she cites King as saying, "the odds are good that people are gonna turn around and cream me" (10). In Shapiro's words, this tendency relates to the age-old dilemma of commercial success vs. fine art; the twain rarely meet. King's brand of kink and kineticism has brought him a popular success that's rivaled by very few, but there are killjoys out there who feel that 'mass culture' is a contradiction in terms. No one is as keenly aware of this as King: in fact, I've never heard someone so finely attuned to his own drawbacks, so spot-on about the repercussions of the limelight. (10)

In a forthright conclusion to the discussion, King talks about his fears for *The Talisman*, including the sense that critics would savage it because he and Straub were too successful: "When you get too big and too many people like your stuff it must be mediocre. A mass mind is supposedly ordinary, not sensitive, literate and smart like the mind of a critic. Of course, it's possible to dismiss all criticism by saying they're just jealous" (10). He does, however, listen to critics; and he is aware of his faults as a writer—that his work is derivative, some of it is simplistic, and that he's not "an original thinker." On the plus side, he attempts to overcome more of these problems with each new novel.

Still, his understanding and openness did not help when *Maximum Overdrive* was released. It was not just a flawed film, according to many of the reviews available—it was a *personal* failure for Stephen King. Larry Ratliff begins his consideration of the film with the confusing assertion that "While it may be some consolation to Stephen King, this generation's one-man horror gristmill, 'Maximum Overdrive' only proves that the author himself can turn gore into bore just about as well as more experienced directors." The film is a short story padded to "an excruciating 97 minutes"; it is a "clunker"; King's promises to "scare the hell out of us" turn into King "grinding gears . . . even for his type of audience—the kind who think it's incredibly 'cool' to watch a movie with feet propped on seats in front of them." The review concludes by comparing *Maximum Overdrive* with the "ultimate 'truck run amok' film," Steven Spielberg's *Duel* (1971), even though there is little evidence that the two were intended to be compared.

What emerges from the review is not so much an assessment of a film as an implied critique of Stephen King, of his chosen genre, and of his status as a best-selling writer.

Robert Garrett begins his discussion of *Maximum Overdrive* by calling it a "factory reject," its narrative flawed by a "comic book-style [sic] idiocy that at times is charming." King's debut as a director is "boneheadedly direct and banal", resulting in a situation that is a "pale reminder of the beleaguered townies who hid in a diner in *The Birds*, although the tiniest of Hitchcock's sparrows is spookier than King's big wheelers."

It is well and good to compare King's first film to Spielberg and Hitchcock and find it wanting; what Ratliff and Garrett seem to have ignored is King's own assessment of the film. He has frequently called it a "moron movie," meaning that

> it isn't a serious picture. You can go to the theater, sit down with a box of popcorn and a drink and believe everything you see for the next two hours. It isn't a serious movie in any way. Just leave your brains outside. (Louka, 11)

In another response to the "moron film" reference, King simply said:

> This movie is about having a good time at the movies, and that's all it's about. Believe me, it's not 'My Dinner With Andre.' And little Stevie is not rehearsing his Academy Award speech for *this* baby. (Burkett, H1)

Even such disclaimers did not assuage one reviewer, who noted that King had called it a "moron movie," but that he had overestimated its effect.

Early reactions to *Stand by Me* also indicate King's difficulties. The film was superbly directed by Rob Reiner, who made several changes in King's original narrative, even commenting that "Stephen's novella was set in 1960, but since I was twelve in 1959, we moved it back a year, because the references seemed even more natural to me. The film became a blend of Stephen's story and mine. . . . The film only came into focus after I made my own personal connections to it" (Holden, C8). The screenplay was written by Reynold Gideon and Bruce A. Evans, who, with Andrew Scheinman, also produced the film.

King's contribution to *Stand By Me* was thus diluted as the material passed through several hands; in fact, it seems probable that King's connections with the original narrative were purposely downplayed. Daniel Cziraky notes that "as bankable as King's name has become in the publishing world, the poor performance of past films based on his works was most likely a very big factor in Columbia's releasing the film as 'Stand By Me,' 'A Rob Reiner Film,' instead of Stephen King's 'The Body.'" While such thinking might be logical, Cziraky writes, it has the unfortunate side effect of distancing King from the finest film adaptation of his works yet produced.

In spite of that distancing, however, a number of reviewers seem intent on bringing King into the discussion. Generally speaking, according to several early reviewers, where the film succeeds it shows Reiner's hand; where it fails, it shows King's. Rex Reed disliked the film, noting that "rarely have 90 minutes of screen time been devoted to anything more trivial or pointless." He carefully includes the comment that the film was based on a story by King, "who publishes everything but his grocery list and calls it literature"—a comment that may have some validity in terms of King's reputation as a writer but seems to have little direct bearing on a film several steps removed from King's prose. The implication is that the film is suspect simply because of its relation to Stephen King.

Kevin Lally finds the film much stronger, a "delightful sleeper," a "raucously appealing portrait of 12-year-olds." Yet he also insists that the underlying narrative is atypical of King, improved by strong directing by Reiner and equally strong writing by Gideon and Evans. Overall, the review is positive and helpful—until Lally feels it necessary to discuss King directly. *Stand By Me* is told from the point of view of Gordon Lachance, a successful writer:

> But if Gordie is meant to be King's alter ego, his pensive style gives no clue that it belongs to someone who's made his fortune from pulpy, grundgy horror stories.
>
> Still, the one yarn young Gordie tells his friends—about a fat boy's disgusting revenge on his hometown—is in tune with the King that America has taken to heart."

King's novella might have seemed to portray Lachance as "King's alter ego," particularly since the two stories interpolated into "The Body" were in fact juvenalia by King; he is himself aware of the suggested connection, as is evidenced by a comment in a letter discussing *IT* that "Derry is no more Bangor than Gordie Lachance is the young Steve King" (31 March 1986).

Stand By Me is even less transparent in this regard than was "The Body." The film's Gordie seems to reflect Rob Reiner as much Stephen King: "The feelings Gordie expresses in the film were very much like the feelings I've had for most of my life," Reiner said in an interview (Holden, C8). Lally's attempt to find King within the film, and, subsequently to use that discovery as a springboard for a negative statement about King's writing career, seems gratuitous and unfair to King, to Reiner, and to the film.

Richard Freedman uses the same technique in his review: the film is strong because of Reiner, weak when it depends on King's narrative. "Considering what a disaster Stephen King's 'Maximum Overdrive' is," Freedman begins,

> directed by the best-selling horror novelist himself, it's a pleasure to report that "Stand By Me," based on his novella "The Body,"

is an almost unqualified success.

But then it's directed by Rob Reiner . . . , as skilled behind the camera as King is a seemingly hopeless duffer.

Later, Freedman details several weaknesses in the film:

Poorest of all, there's a kind of pity and self-aggrandizement on the part of the author that nearly spoils the tone of this dark idyll:

"You're going to be a great writer some day, Gordie," Chris tells him, and one can just see King licking his chops as he set that line down (actually, in all fairness, the screen adaptation is by co-producers Raynold Gideon and Bruce A. Evans, but would Tolstoy have been capable of such self-preening fatuity?) . . .

The parenthetical comment is itself confusing, since it seems at once to accuse King and to expiate him—and why the reference to Tolstoy in the first place? Nor, in the context of the film, is Chris's line out of place. Gordie has just confessed his deepest fears—that his father hates him, that he is no good—and Chris comforts him by admiring the one talent the film has clearly established that Gordie possesses: his ability to tell stories. At least three times prior to this scene, Chris has complimented Gordie on that skill; what better way to build up the younger boy's shattered self-image. To charge King with intruding "pity and self-aggrandizement" into the film works against the nature of *Stand By Me*.

The film is strong—with *Dead Zone* and *The Woman in the Room* among the most successful adaptations, with a fine screenplay and sensitive, careful directing. But to remove King from the equation entirely is as unfair as to blame him for every infelicity in the film. Yet many of the strongest responses to *Stand By Me* did precisely that.

Sheila Benson wrote in the Los Angeles *Times* that the film was the "summer's great gift, a compassionate perfectly formed look at the real heart of youth." She commends the writers, the actors, and especially the director: Reiner "has seen that the cast stays honest and his movie marvelously restrained." There is no mention at all of Stephen King.

Tom Cuneff does refer to King, but in the opening sentence, and then by way of establishing one condition for the film's success: "Though this movie is based on a novella . . . by scaremeister Stephen King, it's not just another one of his chillers." The remainder of the review is perceptive and positive, but ignores King.

Similarly, David Brooks's review concentrates on Reiner, on the narrative, on the actors, and on the relationships among the characters, but mentions King only once, in a paragraph that sounds a familiar chord: "Who could have predicted that a movie, let alone a very good movie, could be made from a story about four 12-year-olds hiking to find a dead boy? Set in 1959 and based on Stephen King's novella 'The Body,' 'Stand By Me' is an author's remembrance of his pivotal childhood adventure." The author in question is not even King; Brooks's next sentence speaks of Gordie Lachance, not Stephen King.

In the cases of *Maximum Overdrive* and *Stand By Me*, King's reputation is an almost impossible barrier to overcome. One film apparently failed because of King; the second succeeded in spite of him.

The situation with King criticism in general is equally diverse. In "King of Horror," Robert Hunt prefaces his discussion of film adaptation by arguing that

> King is the Steven Spielberg of horror. Like Spielberg, he's obsessed with popular culture, and particularly with those parts of it which he grew up watching: King would like to believe that his taste and sensibility have remained unchanged since the seventh grade. No pop culture revisionist, King deals with horror archetypes: if he writes about a vampire, you can be sure he won't leave out the coffin, the stake, or the garlic; his werewolf, likewise, will be destroyed only by a silver bullet during a full moon. But King also recognizes that his subjects are archetypal, and knows just how much distance to keep from them. He knows his horror traditions, and knows better than to take them too seriously. (40)

Yet Hunt follows this paragraph with the disclaimer that he is referring only to the plots in the film adaptations; he has read few of King's novels, he admits, and those were "uninteresting stylistically." *Carrie* was a pot-boiler, a "routine entry in the then popular cycle of books about possessed kids" (40); *Cujo* is silly, and *Christine* even sillier, with the film's few impressive moments the result of John Carpenter moving away from King's "hot-rod version of *Carrie*" toward an emphasis on human characters. *Cat's Eye* succeeds better than did *Creepshow*, although largely because the later film is "perhaps the sort of thing that King . . . does best: simple, slightly familiar suspense situations that don't take themselves too seriously" (42). The point of Hunt's extensive analyses seems to be that the films are superior to the novels; yet even in discussing the films, Hunt carefully identifies King's failings as a writer.

Many reviews of King's novels have paralleled these attitudes. *Kirkus Reviews* (15 August 1975) referred to *'Salem's Lot* as "super-exorcism that leaves the taste of somebody else's blood in your mouth and what a bad taste it is. . . . Vampirism, necrophilia, *et* dreadful *alia* rather overplayed. . . . "

Jack Sullivan's "Ten Ways to Write a Gothic," appearing in the *New York Times Book Review* in February, 1977, takes King severely to task for stylistic blunders: "To say Stephen King is not an elegant writer . . . is putting it mildly." He particularly dislikes King's use of parentheses, capitals and exclamation marks as points of emphasis in *The Shining*: "Sometimes non-punctuation or italics are used—quite arbitrarily—for gimmicky stream of consciousness effect." In addition, the novel's plot is obviously a re-working of Poe, Blackwood, and Lovecraft, as well as such films as *Diabolique*, *Psycho*, and the *Village of the Damned*; perhaps Sullivan might have discussed such internal referents as "allusions" in another writer, but for some reason, King is not allowed the liberty of building on the literary past, even though he acknowledges his debt to that past throughout the novel.

Michael Mewshaw similarly attacked King as stylist in "Novels and Stories," which also appeared in the *New York Times Book Review* (26 March 1978). The *Night Shift* stories may be imaginative, but they suffer from "twist endings that should have died with O. Henry, the hoariest cliches of the horror-tale subgenre . . . and lines that provoke smiles rather than terror."

Eight years later, King's most ambitious novel has come in for a similar drubbing. John Podhoretz's review of *IT*, "Stopping 'It' Before It's Too Late," is written as a parody of the novel itself, with four parts and a narrative tone and style clearly based on King's own:

> *It can't be, it just can't be*, he thought wildly, *not again, not SO SOON*! He was quaking in his Nocona boots. For there, sitting right there, as though God or the devil
> *(it's the latter oh God it's the latter oh I know it's the devil)*
> had placed it there, was a gigantic book with a dark painting on the cover, and in large red type, the word "It." (68)

The article continues in this vein, criticizing the novel (as King had predicted) for its length: 1,138 pages (the hardcover *Stand* is only 823 pages long). As early as the *Adelina* reviews, King noted that as far as mainstream critics were concerned, the long novel had died long ago, and that since the 1950s, novels were more and more frequently discriminated against on the basis of length alone. "Many critics," he noted in 1980, "seem to take a novel of more than 400 pages as a personal affront." As evidence, he cites negative responses to *The Dead Zone* ("One critic was so put out by [its] length . . . that he wished I might contract a case of permanent dyslexia") and *The Stand* (King cites one comment to the effect that "Given enough rope, any writer will hang himself . . . and in this novel, King has taken enough rope to outfit an entire clipper ship") (King, "Love Those Long Novels" 9).

It was not surprising, then, that King would anticipate even more negative responses to *It* largely on the basis of its length. In one letter, he noted sadly that "the days when *any* novel as long as this gets much of a critical reading are gone" (31 March, 1986). In a lighter vein, he acknowledged the difficulty of reading such a massive work. After seeing the entire manuscript in a single stack, he writes, "a Great Postulate occurred to me: no manuscript weighing more than twelve pounds can *possibly* be any good. I also made my first New Year's Resolution in some ten years that night: *Never write anything bigger than your own head*" (Letter, 3 March 1986).

King was, therefore, prepared to some extent for reactions such as Podhoretz's to *It*, at least as far as the novel's length is concerned.

Podhoretz found more to quibble with in the novel than mere length, however. *It* demonstrates all of King's trademarks: a setting in Maine; quotations from rock songs; blood and gore; brand names; geographical accuracy to tie its horrors to the real world; "real get-down-in-the-gutter-and-sound-like-an-illiterate-moron-writing" set next to passages of more self-consciously elevated prose. The latter criticism sounds much like Mark Twain's condemnation of James Fenimore Cooper's literary offenses.

In despair, Podhoretz consults his own Von Helsing, a certain Dr. Smith, a mild-mannered University English professor by day and researcher into the occult by night. Smith warns Podhoretz that King must be stopped: "If you don't, this will go on forever. He'll publish longer and longer books. Two, three thousand pages. Five thousand. Your life will be devoted to reading his books. You will quit your job, you'll have no money, and you'll starve to death" (69).

The result is a quick trip to Maine, where Podhoretz confronts King to define the ultimate failure of *It*—it is boring. It depends upon the banality of blood, upon extensive passages of cruelty to create the interest that its implicit horror-elements cannot. King is no longer scary, Podhoretz asserts, so he had to fall back on unpleasantness (apparently ignoring King's claims that unpleasantness—what King refers to as the "gross out"—is inherent in King's theory of horror).

Not that King was always such, Podhoretz adds; once, in fact, he was a master of sorts—but Podhoretz carefully undercuts the positive with the negative. *The Stand* was a great novel, he says, adding the derogatory "in its own pulpy way":

"The Shining" was genuinely imaginative and "'Salem's Lot" the only vampire novel worthy of comparison to "Dracula."

But now where are you? You're hoping that prolixity will accomplish what your imagination can't. (69)

With *It*, King has given up on the supernatural and hopes to frighten by sheer bulk and page count. The novel is boring, King is boring, and Podhoretz warns that if this sort of thing continues, King will lose his fans.

There are, of course, positive reviews of *IT*—many of them. But even there, a certain oddly lingering reticence attaches itself, often in unusual ways. The Los Angeles *Times Book Review* included a strongly favorable piece on the novel:

> I wait for each new King novel as an alcoholic waits for the next drink. I am addicted. If you are not, I suggest you introduce yourself to King's work through one of his earlier novels— "Carrie" or "The Shining." If, however, you are already a King addict, "It" will overwhelm you. (Goldberg 2)

The difficulty lies not so much in what is said (although the review is essentially plot summary rather than evaluation) as in who says it: Whoopi Goldberg, whose listed credentials are restricted to her work in film and theater. While she certainly has a right to an attitude toward King and King's novels, it unfortunately seems possible that her assignment to review the book was as much a mark of her reputation as a Hollywood personality as of her literary expertise.

This emphasis on personality leads to another form of popular criticism, which tends to ignore the works themselves and concentrate on *King* as personality—generally to his detriment. G. Wayne Allen begins his discussion of *Maximum Overdrive*, not with references to the film but by describing King:

> Stephen King, the most popular horror writer of all time, is eating pizza—thick, oily, mega-calorie pizza with all the fixings. He's eating it the way a big hungry kid would—ferociously and noisily. Stephen King loves pizza, just as he loves scaring the pants off people.
>
> King, who has made enough money from what he calls a "marketable obsession" to buy Brooks Brothers' entire inventory, is dressed in jeans, work shirt, running shoes. Comfort is the thing for King, who sets many of his stories in rural Maine, the place he's lived for most of his 38 years.

Would his visitor like a slice of that greasy, monster masquerading as a pizza, he asks politely? No? Then have a seat. Feel at home.

He sits—flops is probably a better word—onto an oversized chair in his hotel suite. King is well over six feet tall, and his long legs seem to stretch halfway across this elegantly furnished sitting room. He brushes his black hair off his face, grins mischievously, and peers from behind thick glasses, his "Coke bottles," as he's referred to them. (I–1)

Nothing in the passage seems directly relevant to *Maximum Overdrive* as film; everything, instead, points to Stephen King as eccentric celebrity.

For another writer, what seems most important is King's "long lantern-jawed face framed by a jet black bowl of hair that rises in two sweeping arcs around his forehead like the drooping wings of some bat" (Beeber 16A); for yet another, it is the hamburger he eats on the set of *Maximum Overdrive*, a greasy hamburger dripping with blood-like catsup.

The problem is, of course, that it is difficult to see exactly what his pizza and hamburger and hairstyle have to do with the quality of his writing or directing—and yet they are treated as if they were of paramount importance. John Coyne was speaking of this sort of pseudo-criticism, criticism by personality, when he commented that King was becoming his "own worst enemy"; Stephen King the writer was being replaced by Stephen King the visible personality. "You really shouldn't be known," Coyne says.

J. D. Salinger has probably sold a lot more copies just because no one knows who J. D. Salinger is. If King or I wanted to play this game really well, we would be totally anonymous. We would be sending books in via UPS. King's problem—and it's a problem for all of us—is, what if he wants to write a love story? If he writes under his own name, he'll disappoint his readers, because they're expecting, if nothing else, that one lover will chop off the other's head or whatever. (Winter, "Coyne" 13–14)

In King's case, it has progressed even beyond that sort of disappointment. Now, a novel or film must live up to the media hype, and up to the popular image of King himself as the "titan of terror" and the "king of horror," and up to the impossible expectations generated by over thirty books and seventeen film adaptations in fewer than thirteen years.

Paradoxically, because of his popular and commercial successes it becomes more and more difficult for King to attain critical success.

2. ACADEMIC CRITICISM

Thus far, I have concentrated only on one sort of criticism—what might be called mainstream, non-academic, and popular criticism—and one sort of reaction to King.

There are, of course, others.

Academic critics have discovered King and are in many cases working diligently to place King within the framework of an acknowledged traditional literary heritage. In spite of references to such critical and scholarly endeavors as fostering a "cottage industry," collections of essays, such as Darrell Schweitzer's *Discovering Stephen King* (1985) and Underwood and Miller's *Fear Itself: The Horror Fiction of Stephen King* (1982; 1984) and *Kingdom of Fear: The World of Stephen King* (1986), include a number of valuable studies: Gary William Crawford's "Stephen King's American Gothic"; Robert M. Price's "Stephen King and the Lovecraft Mythos"; Debra Stump's "A Matter of Choice: King's *Cujo* and Malamud's *The Natural*"; Leonard Heldreth's "The Ultimate Horror: The Dead Child in Stephen King's Stories and Novels"; Bernadette Bosky's "The Mind's a Monkey: Character and Psychology in Stephen King's Recent Fiction"; and Ben P. Indick's "King and the Literary Tradition of Horror and the Supernatural."

One particularly useful piece, Michael McDowell's "The Unexpected and the Inevitable," begins by disparaging the "sapping methods of literary 'appreciation' taught in colleges and graduate schools," then proceeds to demonstrate graphically and convincingly King's mastery of pacing and rhythm. McDowell's chapter in *Kingdom of Fear* not only elucidates an important element in King's appeal to readers, but simultaneously provides an example of literary criticism that makes a difference for the readers.

Other articles on King have found their ways into periodicals—scholarly and academic journals not devoted to King studies or even to horror literature. James Egan's "'A Single Powerful Spectacle': Stephen King's Gothic Melodrama" appeared in the Spring 1986 issue of *Extrapolation*, a journal dedicated to understanding science fiction and fantasy. The article concentrates on King's relationship to a literary thread extending from Mary Shelley through Bram Stoker, Henry James, and Shirley Jackson, concluding that "King's treatment of the Gothic and the macabre are the opposite of impulsive meanderings—he consistently seeks to create a 'single powerful spectacle'" within a tradition that "has existed from the beginnings of literary history" (74). Two years earlier, Egan published "Apocalypticism in the Fiction of Stephen King," also in *Extrapolation*; in the same year *Clues: A Journal of Detection* published his "Antidetection: Gothic and Detective Conventions in the Fiction of Stephen King." In 1986, Gary William Crawford's new journal *Gothic* published Kenneth Gibbs's "Stephen King and the Tradition of American Gothic," a study of King in the context not only of Stoker, Poe, James, and Hawthorne but also of Herman Melville. Karen McGuire's "The Artist as Demon in Mary Shelley, Stevenson, Walpole, Stoker, and King," including an extensive discussion of Ben Mears in *'Salem's Lot*, appeared in the same issue.

This is not to argue that King has reached academic "respectability" as yet—or even that he wishes to do so. There are sufficient reactions to scholarly articles on King as fostering a "cottage industry," and to "instant criticism," that suggest academe still views the man and his critics with a jaundiced eye.

Gary K. Wolfe's review-article in *Modern Fiction Studies*, for example, attempted an overview of recent scholarship in science fiction and fantasy. The pages devoted to King criticism argue that Winter's *Stephen King: The Art of Darkness* is the "only book on Stephen King anyone really needs" (148). The comment sets aside the fact that Winter's book is admittedly more of an appreciation than a critical or scholarly approach to King; in spite of its many excellences, it lacks a certain balance of perception and occasionally overstates its arguments. Gary Crawford, for instance, concludes his own critical overview of horror and the literature of the supernatural by noting that King has been the object of several studies, including Winter's. "Winter's book" is sound," Crawford argues, "but one would think from reading it that King is another Shakespeare; his praise is unqualified" (103).

Still, what is most frustrating about Wolfe's essay is not his singling out an individual volume, but his general attitude toward King and King criticism as a whole. The essay approaches its stated subject, science fiction and fantasy, with a certain seriousness of tone that does Wolfe justice; certainly his discussions of the backgrounds to SF criticism and of such eminent figures in the field as Thomas Clareson, J. G. Ballard, and Philip José Farmer are carefully constructed and effectively argued.

Only with King does Wolfe allow the level of his discourse to alter. "As everyone knows," Wolfe writes,

> there are eight hundred zillion copies of King's books in print, which if lined up end-to-end would free up a considerable amount of shelf space in your local B. Dalton's. (147–148)

Later, in discussing the Starmont series, Wolfe uses such phrases as "flush on the heels of what must have been its greatest success," to comment that Starmont is "brandishing at us not one or two but seven more books about

Stephen King!" On the basis of three, Wolfe feels able to comment on the entire series—and states so specifically.

The difficulty here is that almost everything related to King and horror fiction is treated with an entirely different tone than that which characterizes the rest of the essay. Colloquialisms, exaggerations, exclamations, italicized phrases suggest an underlying attitude not only toward the critics and their writings but toward King himself.

The uncomfortable fact is that King criticism is occasionally as suspect among academics as King's novels are. Certainly that is not the case everywhere; and equally certainly much of the academic establishment's antagonism toward King is softening. Yet the fact remains that many academic writers do not read King, have never read King, have no inclination to ever read King—much less spend time on critical studies.

On the more positive side, King has participated in scholarly conferences, notably the fifth International Conference on the Fantastic in the Arts, held at Boca Raton, Florida, March 22–25, 1984. King served as Guest of Honor, delivering a lecture later published in *Fantasy Review* (June 1984) as "Dr. Seuss and the Two Faces of Fantasy." Even more noteworthy for this discussion, he was the subject of a double session of academic papers chaired by Leonard G. Heldreth of Northern Michigan University at Marquette. The papers presented included "Stephen King's Vietnam Allegory: An Interpretation of 'Children of the Corn,'" by Anthony S. Magistrale of the University of Vermont, Burlington; "The Destruction and Re-Creation of the Human Community in Stephen King's *The Stand*," by Burton Hatlen, King's former professor at the University of Maine at Orono; "Stephen King's *The Stand*: Science Fiction into Fantasy," by Michael R. Collings of Pepperdine University; "Strawberry Spring: Stephen King's Gothic Universe," by Mary Ferguson of the University of Georgia, Athens; and "Monster Love; or Why Is Stephen King?" by Dennis O'Donovan of Florida Atlantic University. Several of the presentations were subsequently published; at least one first appeared in a scholarly quarterly and was then reprinted in a small-press fan publication. In general, the responses to King at this session indicate the range and scope of the more positive academic responses to his work.

Finally, in terms of serious literary responses to King, the Starmont series has attempted to indicate some possibilities for King criticism. Beginning with *Discovering Stephen King* and *Stephen King as Richard Bachman* (1985), each volume has explored a particular facet of King's works: pseudonymous novels, short stories, novels, films produced from King's fictions, and—in this volume—some extra-literary considerations in dealing with King and his reputation. The volumes are not specifically academic;

they are, instead, intended for serious readers of King who might benefit from discussions, backgrounds, and generalized analysis. In addition, they try to bridge the often too-apparent gap between academic criticism and general readership by approaching King from two directions: first, by showing that the standards of traditional and contemporary literary criticism might be justifiably and beneficially applied to King's writings; and second, by showing readers that some familiarity with those standards may be helpful in appreciating and understanding more fully King's achievements.

3. Criticism within the Genre: Appreciations, Peer Criticism, and Fan Responses

On yet another level, some readers respond with personal, gut reactions, often displaying unalloyed adoration—one fan referred to the "orgasmic" experience of reading King's novels. Among fans, for example, criticism emphasizes what the individual reader felt while immersed in the works; there is in general less concern for establishing literary criteria for success or failure.

Paradoxically, Winter's *Stephen King: The Art of Darkness* to a degree falls within this category, since it is an appreciation and biography, coupled with literary criticism that emphasizes psychology and symbolism as well as King's own background. Winter's study has been justifiably influential in interesting readers and writers in King; much of the secondary work done since 1982 depends upon questions Winter posed, evaluations he made, assertions he brought forth. The book represents a fine blend of the fan and the academic, although given Winter's credits as a contributing editor for *Fantasy Review* he might lean more toward fan than academic.

Unfortunately, the dichotomy perceived by many as existing between fan response and academic criticism is rarely so neatly resolved. In an intriguing article published in *Castle Rock: The Stephen King Newsletter*, Christopher Spruce seemed intent on tackling the arbitrary definition of "literature" as "whatever college students study in literature classes, the works having been so deemed by a panel of self-appointed literary experts— usually college professors." Placing King in the context of contemporary American writers, including John Irving, Norman Mailer, and John Updike, Spruce wonders why King is simply disregarded as a writer of horror pulps who has committed the worst possible crime: he sells too many books.

Spruce's discussion is clear up to the point where he refers to those King works that he would nominate as true "literature": "The Reach" and *'Salem's Lot*. His judgment is not particularly the issue here; both are strong works, and "The Reach" does touch on important archetypal and mythic chords.

The difficulty is that, after carefully breaking down the barriers separating King from "good literature," the article then evaluates these two works from a rather fannish perspective. The discussion of "The Reach" concentrates on plot summary and personal response; Spruce empathizes with Stella Flanders because she reminds him of many elderly women he has known in Maine and because she represents a certain sort of character that appeals to him. "Beyond that," he writes in the final paragraph devoted to the story, "my literary senses tell me that this is as good a story as I probably am ever going to have the pleasure of reading" (4).

What is missing is a clear discussion of *why* the story succeeds, not only as entertainment but as literature. And that is the point missing in many fan responses. Adulation is there, but without careful discussion and definition of relevant literary criteria; what is there besides the reader's "literary senses" that demonstrates King's mastery of language and form. Frequently, responses at this level concentrate on story line and on the sensation of fear King's stories and novels produce. These are certainly valid responses (and just as certainly not the only ones possible). The many appreciations, reviews, letters, and informal articles published in *Castle Rock: The Stephen King Newsletter*, for example, go far toward establishing the extent of King's popularity and the depth to which his works are capable of touching readers, regardless of the opinions of mainstream reviewers or academic critics.

As in so many other ways, King remains controversial when it comes to critics and criticism. This chapter represents only an overview of possibilities; it does not pretend to a definitive treatment of the issue. *The Annotated Guide to Stephen King* lists several hundred secondary works relating to King and his writing; each approaches the subject from a different critical and personal stance; each illuminates a slightly different perspective on the man and his works; and each defines for itself the importance—or lack of importance—King holds in contemporary American culture.

JONATHAN P. DAVIS

The Struggle for Personal Morality in America

Before we begin to explore Stephen King's America, I wish to acknowledge the several people whose contributions and inspirations made the journey possible:

My mother and father, John and Barbara Davis, whose undying support of me gave birth to the perseverance needed to complete projects such as this one.

My brothers, Christopher and Andrew, who both tolerate (sometimes) the sound of a computer keyboard in the late hours of the night and who are enthusiastic about Stephen King because of my enthusiasm.

Courtney Gardner, who had been there through thick and thin with support and all the right suggestions.

My buddy, Joe Arrigo, my partner in horror-fiction gluttony.

North Central College, Naperville, Illinois, for having the open-mindedness to reward such a project with scholarship funds.

Dr. Fran Navakas, who through her guidance and willingness to knead through the stacks of manuscript is as much a part of this as I am.

Shirley Sonderegger, Stephen King's secretary, whose hospitality and friendly role as go-between made corresponding with the King office a great pleasure.

From *Stephen King's America*. © 1994 Bowling Green State University Press. Reprinted with permission.

Tony Magistrale, whose zeal for my project prompted him to invite me out to Vermont to participate in his class, swap ideas, and conduct an interview (Thanks Tony!).

Carroll Terrell, who gave a great interview and plenty of laughs.

Burton Hatlen, for his great insight and interest in my project.

Gary Hoppenstand, a gentleman and a scholar, whose contribution and excitement for Stephen King's fiction has spawned a meaningful friendship.

The late Ted Dikty, Starmont House, whose interest during the initial drafting stages provided the catalyst.

Bowling Green State University Popular Press, the medium that brought my passion for the subject to fruition.

And finally, Stephen King, whose love for life and writing has given me the greatest inspiration of all.

I. THE STRUGGLE FOR PERSONAL MORALITY IN AMERICA

In the majority of his fiction, Stephen King seems to understand that while the world is broken up into societies and cultures for the sake of organization, individual people themselves are the driving forces behind change. An analytical interpretation of the human condition in King's fiction must begin with and focus on the individuals that join together to form larger collective bodies. After all, at the center of each and every issue facing people today is a question of moral choice: is it right to dump chemical wastes into streams and lakes? Is it right to abort an unborn child, and, if so, is it or is it not murder? Is it right to let one's sixteen-year-old daughter go on a weekend ski-trip with her boyfriend? Should one slip a candy bar in his pocket if no one is looking? The list of choices that call morality into play are endless. All of these questions have been subjectively called into debate in each and every American's mind, and they all center around the simple differentiation between right and wrong. While evil is a mainstay in the human heart, the magic of the human condition rests in its capacity to do good in spite of the adversities that prompt evil action. At the center of all things that result from human interference is the need to question what is right and what is wrong. It is the answers to these questions that have the largest impact on the human condition.

The appeal of King's fiction to his readers rests in the fact that it constantly raises the question of morality; it recognizes the pervasiveness of evil, but it also aims to prove that the forces of good, when formed behind a collaboration of human hearts to enforce good, will almost always reign over evil. It is only when the protagonists of King's stories alienate themselves from fellow human beings in their battles against evil while failing to recognize their own human flaws that they fall—a notion that reinforces the idea of strength in numbers, that the emphasis in a peaceful human condition is grounded in the collective will to do good. In other words, progress begins with the individual, but there must be a union of good will in order for the human race to further itself. This romantic notion of the potential good residing in the human heart is something that critic Deborah Notkin believes gives King his popular draw:

> Stephen King has achieved unprecedented popularity as a writer of horror fiction, largely because he understands the attraction of fantastic horror to the denizen of the late 20th century, and because, paradoxical though it may sound, he has reassurance to bring us. For whether he is writing about vampires, about the death of 99 percent of the population, or about innocent little girls with the power to break the earth in half, King never stops emphasizing his essential liking for people. He does not, of course, paint a rosy picture of a loving and flawless human race; he simply focuses, again and again, on people doing the right things in difficult situations, on people who behave slightly better than we expect. The overwhelming impression to be gained from reading King's books is that the kinks and the sadists are the exception, not the rule. In these novels, the average person is reasonably honest, caring and upright, and can be relied upon in most circumstances—not a fashionable concept, these days, but one which has obvious attractions for contemporary audiences. (232)

King's power in his fiction is an adamant belief in a personal moral code; those who behave morally and make correct moral choices when faced with adversities are those who are likely to win the fight against evil. Those characters in King's fiction who do not behave morally and rather surrender the well-being of others for evil or selfish motives are those who are ultimately destroyed. *Needful Things* is a prime reference of his idealized moral code. In the novel, entrepreneur Leland Gaunt opens shop in the town of Castle Rock. The name of his shop, Needful Things, is a primary indication of what is stored inside; his inventory consists of those material objects that each resident of Castle Rock most desires. As Gaunt predicts, Castle Rock's residents are willing to pay almost any price for their fancies. Gaunt's price includes two parts—a sum of money, and, most importantly, a trick to be played on a person of his selection. Each and every patron who steps through the door of Needful Things is faced with a moral choice:

should they refuse access to the objects they desperately want and deny the risk of injuring their peers, or should they jump at the offer, abandoning any notion of brotherhood for the sake of personal gain? Unfortunately, most choose the latter, augmenting the mistrust among neighbors that had already been breeding prior to Gaunt's grand opening. Castle Rock's agreement to allow Gaunt, who capitalizes on their selfishness to corrupt it, turns neighbor against neighbor until widespread violence reduces the town to ashes. Two Castle Rockians, Polly Chalmers and Sheriff Alan Pangborn, who are engaged in a love affair, are also seduced by Gaunt's 'needful things,' but, after agonizing deliberation, reject his prizes and acknowledge his seductive scheme; their love for each other shines through the dark veil of their selfishness, and they join together against Gaunt. Likewise, Deputy Norris Ridgewick, although having played a major part in Gaunt's grand plan after performing a trick that triggers murder, also atones for his mistake by rushing to the rescue of Alan and Polly when Gaunt confronts them. In the end, Polly, Alan, and Norris are able to survive simply because they value human bonding over selfish motives. As Notkin's passage suggests, the concept of consequences arising from moral choice such as those portrayed in *Needful Things* is far from fresh or imaginative, but it is one that never loses its flavor or appeal with contemporary audiences. Inside the heart of us is a desire to see the selfishly wicked punished; this conviction is adequately exemplified in the real-life case of convicted serial killer Ted Bundy, who raped and tortured dozens of young girls from Florida to Washington. At his execution, when the switch was thrown, an audience standing outside cheered; he who acted selfishly and immorally against his fellow sisters was served his just desserts.

Yet another aspect of King's fiction pertinent to morality and the human condition is that his monsters and villains stem directly from human evil. His readers like to see his antagonists destroyed because they represent the human monsters that live among the real world—Rev. Jim Jones, Richard Speck, Charles Manson, John Wayne Gacy, Richard Ramirez, Jeffrey Dahmer: these are the extreme atrocities and perversions of the human spirit, the extreme examples of the breach in morality that threatens humankind. Burton Hatlen points out that

> while King recognizes that serial killers truly do exist, he suggests that our fascination with them moves them into the same mythic territory where vampires live; and the myths we create about such people tell us as much about ourselves as they do about the psychopathology of sex murderers. Vampires, killer cars, and rubber-coated sex murderers—all crawl out of the "myth-pool in

which we all bathe communally". . . . We, not King, have created these creatures; and he gives them back to us, to tell us something about ourselves. (84)

It may be that society's tendency to glamorize or raise to cult status psychopaths arises from a need to use those evil-doers as barometrical instruments measuring the sanity and morality of those who condemn their actions. An equally effective measuring device, King's fiction often allows readers to point fingers at the villains contained within and to cherish the truth or contemplate the untruth of each individual's morality.

As mentioned, King's fiction serves to argue that society needs a collective good will. However, that collective good will obviously starts at the individual level. While human beings make haste in accusing others of immoral actions, they often ignore consideration of how to obtain their own moral maturity—a paradox that reveals itself often in King's canon. Each one of King's novels portrays a protagonist or group of protagonists who must make moral decisions that will have impact on their fates. Without moral maturity, both people and King's characters suffer from their inability to heed the consequences of moral differentiation, therefore increasing the difficulty to act on behalf of goodness. Bernadette Lynn Bosky, making reference to one of King's most descript portrayals of moral choice, *Pet Sematary*, summarizes this concern of King's when she points out that:

> King realistically presents his characters with the choice of which interior voice to follow and which to silence. The tragedy of *Pet Sematary* is that Louis Creed begins to follow his intuitions only when he should begin to doubt them. His premonition regarding Gage and his visitation from Pascow are dismissed because they do not fit into his materialistic worldview. (231)

Without an individual's ability to make correct moral decisions, adverse conditions often become unavoidable. As Bosky brings to light, the fate of Louis Creed in *Pet Sematary* results from his anger with life for taking away his only son, Gage, who was struck by a semi-trailer truck when trying to cross a busy highway. Creed's reaction to his son's death is to exhume the corpse and bury it an ancient Indian burial ground behind the pet cemetery near his home, a ground that was once sacred to a tribe of Micmac Indians. Creed had already used the sacred ground to bury his cat Churchill, when it was struck by a truck. The cat had come back from the dead, but was not the same cat: its spirit had been removed by the death process. What Louis saw in the resurrected Churchill was not the fluffy cat his daughter, Ellie, was fond of but rather an evil reincarnation. Rather than reviewing the results of the cat's return from the burial site and applying that knowledge to the horrible potential it could have with a human being, Louis ignores his wiser intuition not to play with death but rather confronts fate. What returns from the burial ground is a soiled, evil, blood-thirsty version of his son. Critic Samuel Schuman supports Bosky's observation when he suggests that:

> it should be clear . . . that the thematic center of the novel derives from the clear moral judgment that it is sinful for humans to tamper with mortality. Creed falls, through love, into a sin the mirror opposite of murder: he does not make the living into the dead; he tries to make the dead to live again, and in so doing brings down upon himself and his family a progressive nightmare from which there is no escape. Within a plot of considerable imaginative ambition, King embeds a thematic core which would be gratifying to the most ardent fundamentalist. (113)

It is Creed's inability to make the distinction between the right and wrong courses of action that creates the fall of his subjective world. His fall is correlative with that of Victor Frankenstein—his failure to make the correct moral choice when pursuing a selfish goal brings destruction and sorrow to both him and his family.

Yet another example of a King character who suffers from a lapse in correct moral choice is Harold Lauder, one of the survivors of the flu epidemic in *The Stand*. Harold is a young social outcast much like the characters that find places in almost every King story. Harold is overweight, unattractive, and unable to communicate with other human beings intimately. When he falls in love with Frannie Goldsmith, his older sister's friend who also survived the epidemic, he cannot outwardly tell her of his feelings but rather keeps them trapped in a personal diary. When Frannie falls in love with Stu Redman, Harold's reaction is not to accept defeat but to allow his bitterness against both of them to mount. Frannie, Stu, and the rest of the Free Zone Committee (the representatives of the army of good will established in the post-epidemic world) all try to make Harold a welcome member, but he rejects them. He cannot accept the fact that he is living in a new world, one needing reconstruction because of the massive population reduction from the superflu, and that the new world will give him an opportunity to become something that he never was in his previous life: a working cog in the mechanism of a meaningful society. As Bosky points out, "Harold will not let himself realize that his rejection of hope and change also murders his new, better self before it is born" (229). Harold is put in a position to accept the bond his Free Zone friends offer him or to reject it for the fulfillment of the destruction of the society he resented previously. His choice to reject human bonding in favor of the selfish goals offered by Randall Flagg, the adversary of the Free Zone, leads to Harold's downfall. Bosky supports this when she observes that:

> [one of the] most stunning scenes of "the free will to do evil or deny it" in King's fiction [has] little or nothing to do with the supernatural. Harold Lauder's acceptance of all-consuming hatred in *The Stand* . . . show[s] that no matter how much or little control we have over situations, we always choose whether or not to control our emotional reactions to these situations. (227)

Both Louis Creed and Harold Lauder may be seen as manifestations of real-life moral issues relevant to modern America. Creed's desire to interfere with the natural death process is applicable to the modern-day concerns about death control—euthanasia—while Harold Lauder's refusal to relinquish his rage over past wrongs can be applied to the continuous warring between countries on the national level and individuals on the domestic level. Both Louis and Harold serve to explicate King's interpretation of what happens when people fail to make correct moral decisions.

When readers are evaluating evil in King's books, they must be able to identify both the outright manifestations of evil and the sources of their power. No one can deny that characters like Randall Flagg, Barlow ('*Salem's Lot*), Pennywise the Clown (*It*), Morgan Sloat (*The Talisman*), and George Stark (*The Dark Half*) are purely concentrated evil; readers can reasonably dismiss any notion of moral redemption for these villains. These evil incarnations serve no other purpose than to destroy humanity and cloud their victims' moral discretion with their dark influences. The dark forces in King's fiction almost always derive their power from the weakness and vulnerabilities of their prey; were it not for human imperfections, these entities would not exert the degree of influence that they are able to carry out. In his book *Stephen King, The Second Decade: Danse Macabre to The Dark Half*, written for the Twayne United States Authors Series, Tony Magistrale argues that

> like the Overlook Hotel, the Tommyknockers, Christine, It, and other examples of maleficence in King's world, evil requires some element of human weakness—ignorance, avarice, anger, rejection, indifference, jealousy—as a means for the initial corruption of innocence. (244)

Burton Hatlen follows up on this when he suggests that "I am here proposing that King sees both Good and Evil as primarily subjective and intersubjective phenomena" (88). In other words, Hatlen is assuming that evil in King's fiction is not a sovereign body separate from humanity but rather is often the product of the accumulated negative impulses inside people, the same people who create their own monsters through their inabilities to love each other and act morally.

The tragedies in King's fiction lie not so much in the victims of evil manifestations but in the stories' central characters' tendency to bow to their human shortcomings, allowing evil to flourish. A majority of King's books place the central protagonists in positions to follow their moral or immoral impulses. Those who consider the implications of acting immorally and act accordingly are those who overcome evil; those who succumb to the immediate gratification that evil offers are those who eventually fall. Take the case of Arnie Cunningham in *Christine*. Arnie is another Harold-Lauder-type character who is rejected by his peers because of his peculiarity and unattractive looks. When he finds Christine, a '57 Plymouth Fury, he finds a new identity. He is able to stand up to his tormentors. He starts dating the most beautiful girl in his high school. The car, a symbol of identity in a young person's life, brings Arnie a sense of confidence. Yet while Christine has rewarded him with a fresh identity, she has also turned him into a hostile, self-serving individual. She kills all of those who have done or intend to do Arnie wrong; she brings his evil impulses to a horrifying reality. At first, Arnie is ignorant of Christine's malicious actions. But as the story continues, and Arnie becomes vaguely aware that since Christine has been in his life, people have been suffering, he must decide whether to scrap her, which would save lives and return Arnie to the thoughtful, caring boy he used to be, or to keep her and the self-fulfilling promises she offers him. Arnie makes his decision in the following scene:

> In fact there were times when he didn't want the car at all. There were times when he felt he would be better off just . . . well, junking it. Not that he ever would, or could. It was just that, sometimes (in the sweaty, shaking aftermath of that dream last night, for instance), he felt that if he got rid of it, he would be . . . happier . . . "Don't worry," Arnie whispered. He ran his hand slowly over the dashboard, loving the feel of it. Yes, the car frightened him sometimes. And he supposed his father was right; it had changed his life to some degree. But he could no more junk it than he could commit suicide. (264)

Arnie is in a position to make a moral choice: trash the car and save both others and himself from her evil, or keep her and continue to feed on the gratifications she can give him. His choice to keep her results in the deaths of several others and ultimately himself.

In another example where moral choice is called to question in King's fiction, Pop Merrill, the pawn shop owner in *The Sun Dog*, a novella in *Four Past Midnight*, has possession of a young boy's Polaroid Sun 660 camera that has caused some unrest due to the recurring picture it takes. Regardless of the person or object the camera is aimed at, the camera continuously produces an image of an angry dog. When Pop and Kevin Delevan, the camera's owner, put the pictures together in succession, it becomes apparent that the dog is turning and moving closer to the front of the picture, looking as though it is preparing to strike. Each successive snapshot brings it nearer until there is no doubt that the dog means to escape and exercise its rage. After becoming aware of the camera's oddity, Pop, a true capitalist, is drawn to its queerness and covets it with the intent of making a profit despite comprehending the implications of potential disaster accompanying it. At one particular point, as the possibility of the dog's intentions becomes more real to Pop, Pop begins to realize that maybe he could do the world and himself a favor by destroying the camera.

> Why not get rid of the camera right here? he thought suddenly. You can. Just get out, walk to the guardrail there, and toss her over. All gone. Goodbye.
>
> But that would have been an impulsive act and Pop Merrill belonged to the Reasonable tribe—belonged to it body and soul, is what I mean to say, He didn't want to do anything on the spur of the moment that he might regret later, and—
>
> If you don't do this, you'll regret it later.
>
> But no. And no. And no. A man couldn't run against his nature. It was unnatural. He needed time to think.
>
> To be sure. (711)

Pop becomes alert to the evil of the camera and is in a position to destroy it, but his choice to keep it for the selfish goals of either uncovering its secrets or reaping the profits of its sale results in his demise. His death comes after snapping the shutter the number of times needed to unleash the monster behind it.

While King often shows that those who reject their better intuitions sometimes fall, he balances his theory of the moral human condition by giving portrayals of heroes who defeat adversity when they choose to act with good will and kindness based on morality. Irv Manders, the old man who offers temporary sanctuary to Andy and Charlie McGee, refugees from a government operation called The Shop, in the novel *Firestarter*, is a prime example. When Andy and his daughter, Charlie, come to Irv's farm while on the run from the agency that plans to apprehend them with the intent of using their supernatural powers for government research, Irv is placed in a situation where he can either recognize their troubles and give them aid or refuse to interfere in the business of others, as many people tend to do, and turn them over to the authorities seeking them. Irv chooses to protect Andy and Charlie and acts on their behalf when The Shop representatives arrive at his home. As Deborah Notkin explains, "Irv seems to personify King's faith, for he can take people on their own recognizance despite contrary evidence, can stand up for their rights as if his own were in jeopardy, and can shelter them without regard for his own danger" (140). It is Irv's refusal to surrender the well-being of Andy and Charlie that serves as an obstacle in The Shop's attempt at apprehension. It is also Irv's selflessness that serves as a reference for the good that may result when one human acts on behalf of another for the remainder of the book. Irv is the extreme opposite of the novel's chief antagonist, John Rainbird, a Shop employee who pretends to be concerned with Charlie but is only misleading her with the intent of winning her trust so that he can get close enough to her to kill her. Irv, on the other hand, is truly interested in her well-being and is willing to sacrifice his own welfare for her. By creating characters like Irv and Rainbird, King offers readers the opportunity to evaluate the two extremes of the moral human condition, and in so doing, allows readers to comprehend the power of good over evil that results from sincere concern for other living creatures. Notkin points out of King, "very few writers of contemporary fiction would even create such a simply good character as Irv Manders, let alone imply that he might be the rule rather than the exception" (141).

While Irv and Rainbird serve to illustrate the scope of moral action arising from a general concern for others, another main cause of King's characters' failure to act morally comes from a combination of their inability to recognize their own shortcomings and their subordination of their human intuition for rational reasoning. These human flaws are innate; it is much easier to rationalize problems by adhering to reason than to trace fault back to the original source, oneself. Only those characters in King's fiction who are able to assert their imperfections can possess the power to change themselves and ultimately act in defense of moral righteousness. Bosky argues that:

> in King's fiction, natural human intuition is almost always correct
> and its results are often positive if followed—which it rarely is by

the adult characters. Many of King's characters consistently refuse to trust their inner hunches, but there is usually at least one character in each story who does follow intuition, often with heroic results and probable, satisfying resolution. (212)

Those characters who acknowledge their weaknesses and trust their inner hunches, the ones innate in promoting the welfare of mankind, are those who acquire the power to fight evil. On the other hand, those characters who forsake intuition for human reasoning are those who are often incapacitated. The reason many of King's characters choose to ignore their intuition is that they have decided to shine a moral searchlight at others when what they really need to do is turn it back toward themselves. They believe in a rational explanation for everything that occurs as dictated by reason and have no faith in human individual choice, more specifically, their own choices. When acting on behalf of reason, they believe they cannot be wrong. Their subjective intuitions and impulses are almost always forfeited and subordinated to rational logic. In King's short story "I Am the Doorway," a story in *Night Shift*, it takes supernatural interference to show the protagonist, Arthur, that he is flawed. During an exploration of Venus, one of Arthur's crewmates ventures outside of the spacecraft. He comes back inside contaminated with an alien presence; that alien presence spreads to Arthur, who recognizes it later with the appearance of several tiny eyes that have been surfacing on his hands. The eyes ultimately force him to look inside of himself from an outsider's point of view:

> It was a feeling like no other in the world—as if I were a portal just slightly ajar through which they were peeking at a world which they hated and feared. But the worst part was that I could see, too, in a way. Imagine your mind transported into a body of a housefly, a housefly looking into your own face with a thousand eyes. Then perhaps you can begin to see why I kept my hands bandaged even when there was no one around to see them. (97–98)

He says, describing the sensation received from the alien eyes in his hands: "But that was not what made me scream. I had looked into my own face and seen a monster" (101). Arthur, a representative of the common human being incapable of recognizing his own faults—one of the "Reasonable tribe"— needs the interference of an outside presence, a presence that is not human, to see that he is imperfect. A character like Arthur serves to reinforce one of King's general concerns about human beings—that personal introspection is sometimes impossible to achieve by oneself; the fact that King must create an outside supernatural force to hold up a moral mirror to Arthur's face should say something about King's recognition of some people's inability to evaluate themselves. Characters like *Pet Sematary*'s Louis Creed, *The Stand*'s Harold Lauder, *The Sun Dog*'s Pop Merrill, and *Christine*'s Arnie Cunningham—characters who aren't fortunate enough to benefit from an outside interference that causes them to question their own morality—are blunt examples of what happens in King's world when humans remain ignorant of their own shortcomings.

King's concept of moral degeneration arising from humans' indifference to their own flaws is not an original one. It is a theme that can be found throughout literature merely because of its universal truth; it does not apply solely to today's people and society but rather addresses the human condition as it has been throughout time. In drawing a comparison between King's protagonists and those created by other significant writers such as Herman Melville and Edgar Allen Poe, Tony Magistrale illustrates the universality of the idea:

> There is a strong suggestion that Ahab and Poe's narrators secretly hate what they see to be a reflection of themselves found in the objects of their vengeance; for it is clear that in abandoning the most fundamental precepts of morality in order to accommodate the selfish urge to dominate and torment their fellow creatures, Ahab and Poe's narrators end up destroying themselves. (LOF 21)

As the passage serves to explicate, the failure of people to successfully investigate their own morality, resulting in a self-destructive projection of internal flaws onto an external embodiment of those flaws, has been recognized by authors for years. In King's canon, the recognition can often be found in his portrayal of an adult world that persecutes its young; King's adults often subliminally despise both the exposure to worldliness and the access to evil brought about by their physical and mental growth, and they project that hatred to those that they no longer are: the young and innocent (*It, The Body, The Library Policeman, The Talisman*). In *Stephen King: The Art of Darkness*, Douglas Winter also points out that moral degeneration from lack of introspection is not an original King concept:

> King's plague of vampires, like that of Jack Finney's "body snatchers," is less an invasion than a sudden confirmation of what we have silently suspected all along: that we are taking over

ourselves, individuals succumbing to the whole. The relentless process of fragmentation and isolation—a progressive degradation of individuals to a one-dimensional, spiritless mass—has seen the moral disintegration of an entire town [regarding *Salem's Lot*]. (47)

What Winter is referring to in citing '*Salem's Lot* is a town of people who are so busy finding faults in their neighbors that they are not able to unite in battle against the vampires that are preying upon them. The novel is not so much about vampires as it is about the fall of a community resulting from a breach of faith among brothers and sisters. King often details in the novel the ludicrousness of the exchanges between '*Salem's Lot*'s citizens. Rather than utilizing their energies to identify and change their own imperfections, they highlight those of others. These tendencies culminate in a state of isolation, denying any form of human bonding in the struggle, culminating in a complete lack of community action. The citizens have not been destroyed by vampires so much as they have destroyed themselves because of their inability to change and correct their own lives through moral maturity.

What English fiction, horror fiction, and specifically Stephen King's fiction have to teach their readers is that the first step toward mental maturity is gaining an understanding of the impact each and every person's moral standing has on the rest of society. As real monsters such as Ted Bundy and Jeffrey Dahmer have shown, even one person's breach of morality can affect the lives of an entire city or nation. Once an individual has learned the consequences of choice, learned to share the self with others, learned to see one's personal shortcomings, learned to believe in the good residing in the human spirit, then he or she will have taken a step toward becoming whole that may be more significant than any other emotional development imaginable. The fictitious characters Stephen King creates serve to present to King's readers images of themselves, calling to question issues of their own morality.

TONY MAGISTRALE

Toward Defining an American Gothic: Stephen King and the Romance Tradition

In a recent edition of my favorite comic strip, "Bloom County," Opus, the obtuse penguin, suffers from a severe case of amnesia. Unable to remember even the most elemental aspects of his personality, he wonders aloud, "Do I prefer spinach salads for lunch? . . . or pistachio-nut ice cream? Do I read Saul Bellow or Stephen King?" The final frame shows Opus at home in a comfortable chair, dipping into a gallon tub of pistachio-nut ice cream and reading an enormous book entitled *The Gore* by Stephen King.

Perhaps better than any other comic strip currently in circulation, "Bloom County" achieves its humor in reflecting and parodying the manners of American popular culture. In the particular episode cited above, pistachio-nut ice cream and the brand-name fame of Stephen King are emblematic of America's junk food culture, while Saul Bellow is paired with the more respectable spinach salad. As the confused Opus acknowledges, pistachio-nut ice cream and Mr. King are clearly distinguished from the more substantial contents available in spinach salads and the fiction of Saul Bellow. King's novels may be more fun to devour than those of Bellow, but they are also perceived as being less significant, less "serious."

Despite an emerging corpus of film and literary criticism in the past few years that has treated King's fiction quite seriously, his long-standing artistic reputation is still considered in doubt. There are several reasons for this, the most frequently ascribed of which probably fall within this list:

From *Landscape of Fear: Stephen King's American Gothic*. © 1988 Bowling Green State University Press. Reprinted with permission.

(1) King makes too much money with his books (at this writing his yearly income is greater than the gross national products of most third world nations) and any popular writer can't be so good as his press;

(2) he produces nearly a book a year, so he must not work very hard at his craft;

(3) his predominant subject themes are the supernatural, the bizarre, and the occult, and he is therefore only tangentially concerned with the realities of contemporary life; and

(4) he needs an editor, presumably because many of his books are overwritten and badly organized.

It should not suffice for an *aficionado* of King's work to dismiss the above points as merely the cynical judgement of English teachers who are underpaid and unimpressed by creatures of the night. King himself has, to varying degrees, addressed each of these complaints in interviews, introductions to his fiction, and in his own analysis of the horror genre, *Danse Macabre*. In all honesty, much of King's *oeuvre* would benefit from the tough advice of a good editor; there are, for example, a number of instances where King's work could be substantially improved as a result of some judicious revising. However, it is both unfair and inaccurate when any or all of these laments serve as the basis for degrading King's importance as a serious American artist. Indeed, one of the primary motivations for the existence of this book is the resolute commitment on the part of its author to enhance the literary reputation—which, as we have seen, is often at odds with a popular one—of Stephen King's fiction by giving it the type of analysis it justly deserves, and for too long has failed to enjoy.

1

Who buys Stephen King's books and why?

In discussing the influence of the sociopolitical atmosphere of the 1950s on the evolution of the horror film, King argues in *Danse Macabre* that his generation represented

> . . . fertile ground for the seeds of terror, we were war babies; we had been raised in a strange circus atmosphere of paranoia, patriotism, and national *hubris*. We were told that we were the greatest nation on earth and that any Iron Curtain outlaw who tried to draw down on us in that great saloon of international politics would discover who the fastest gun in the west was (as in

Pat Frank's illuminating novel of the period, *Alas, Babylon*), but we were also told exactly what to keep in our fallout shelters and how long we would have to stay in there after we won the war. We had more to eat than any nation in the history of the world, but there were traces of Strontium-90 in our milk from nuclear testing. (23)

None of the issues King discusses above has changed much in three decades; the stakes are still high, the missiles more plentiful. The anxiety associated with the realities of modern life leads readers to King. His apocalyptic vision of a world in ruins (*The Stand*) or the nightmare of science unleashed beyond mortal control (*Firestarter*, *The Mist*, and "I am the Doorway") are invented themes bordering on the very edge of possibility. The parallels between the world of King's novels and our own grow increasingly striking as we spin blindfolded toward the twenty-first century. In an age where it sometimes seems that to eat and drink and breathe is to be helplessly inviting cancer; where the constant threat of war in the Middle East and Latin America threatens to escalate into one final conflagration; where instruments of mass destruction increase in capability and sophistication, while those in charge of them seem less responsible and prudent; and where random and purposeless acts of violence have tacitly become an accepted element of Western life, King's fictional plots are appearing less and less surreal. And whether his audience reads to indulge a kind of perverse enchantment in imagining the destruction of humankind, or reads to reaffirm the importance of circumventing Armageddon, King's novels and tales are reminders of how far we as a collective society and culture have strayed from a balanced moral perspective. As a result, his fiction possesses a political and social relevance that is as serious and significant a contribution as anything Saul Bellow has yet to tell us.

King's tendency toward overwriting notwithstanding, his prose style remains deceptively simple and accessible, and the ease with which one of his imaginary worlds envelops the reader represents another reason for his popularity. In reading a novel such as *The Shining* or *Christine*, it is quite possible to withdraw from all commitments to family and friends, re-emerging after two or three days bleary-eyed and perhaps slightly paranoid, but nonetheless aware of having been transported into a fascinating realm. King himself acknowledges this very tendency in an interview he shared with Douglas Winter published in the book *Faces of Fear*:

In most cases, [my] characters seem very open and accessible. They seem like people that you would like to know, or even

people you do know. People respond to that, and there is very
little of that in novels today. . . . In most of the books, I think,
there's a kind of Steve King hammock that you fall into—and you
feel really comfortable in that hammock, because you know these
people and you feel good about them. You don't have unease
about who they are; you have unease about the circumstances
that they find themselves in. And that's where the suspense comes
from. (251)

King's best work employs many of the same techniques found in film,
which is the most obvious explanation why his novels translate so well into
movies. He possesses the ability to maintain levels of suspense because the
imaginary world he portrays is so accurately visual. Consider, for example,
this scene from the short story "The Ledge," a tale in which a jealous
husband, who has discovered his wife's infidelity, torments her lover by
forcing him to walk around the penthouse ledge of a high-rise apartment
building:

I waited for the wind to drop, but for a long time it refused to,
almost as though it were Cressner's willing ally. It slapped against
me with vicious, invisible fingers, prying and poking and tickling.
At last, after a particularly strong gust had made me rock on my
toes, I knew that I could wait forever and the wind would never
drop all the way off.
    So the next time it sank a little, I slipped my right foot around
and, clutching both walls with my hands, made the turn. The
crosswind pushed me two ways at once, and I tottered. For a
second I was sickeningly sure that Cressner had won his wager.
Then I slid a step farther along and pressed myself tightly against
the wall, a held breath slipping out of my dry throat. (190)

In this excerpt we see King's descriptive abilities at their very best. Not
only does the reader clearly visualize the desperate plight of the narrator,
clinging to the building with his legs and hands while the wind's personified
"fingers" pull at his body, but his terrifying situation likewise fills us with pity
and fear. As his journey around the building unfolds, his staccato breaths
become ours, until finally we urge his survival, completely overlook his
infidelity with Cressner's wife, and applaud the ironic conclusion as the
narrator turns the tables on his tormentor and makes him walk the ledge.
    King's many skills and liabilities as a writer are readily apparent. But his
name has been elevated to brand-name status primarily because of his ability

to create supernatural effects. As I will argue elsewhere in this book, I believe these extraordinary occurrences can be traced directly to King's sociopolitical perspective on contemporary America, but this is probably not an affiliation most readers make. As is the case with his general prose style, King's monsters are always highly visual manifestations, whether they occupy the form of rampaging trucks on an interstate highway, a malevolent deity who inhabits the cornfields of Nebraska, or the animated topiary outside a Colorado hotel. Once the reader is introduced to these creatures, he sleeps the worst for it.

King's most loyal readers belong to generations of movie goers who have attended repeated viewing of Lucas' *Star Wars* trilogy, adults and children who were nurtured on television reruns of *The Twilight Zone* and *The Outer Limits*, individuals who have spent entire afternoons transfixed by the human–animal–vegetable hybrids in the paintings of Hieronymus Bosch, and those whose literary tastes remain committed to annual readings of Tolkien's *Lord of the Rings Trilogy*. Several critics, most notably Douglas Winter and Don Herron, have reminded us of King's debt to the book and film success of *Rosemary's Baby* and *The Exorcist*. In the early 1970s these productions revitalized public fascination with the horror genre by focusing on its urban possibilities. Steering deliberately away from the science-fiction backdrops that characterized the genre's major contribution to literature and film in the 1950s and 1960s, Ira Levin's *Rosemary's Baby* and William Blatty's *The Exorcist* bring the terror back down to earth; indeed, their work is a reminder that the darkest evils are always those found in our neighborhoods, in our children, and in ourselves rather than in some deserted place out among the stars. As King reminds us in *Danse Macabre*, "the strongest watchspring of *Rosemary's Baby* isn't the religious subtheme but the book's use of urban paranoia. . . . Our dread for Rosemary springs from the fact that she seems the only normal person in a whole city of dangerous maniacs" (288–9).

King not only capitalized on the immeasurable public interest awarded to *Rosemary's Baby* and *The Exorcist*, as both novels and film adaptations appeared just before King's first publication (*Carrie*, 1974), but he likewise continued to emphasize the horror potential available in the everyday world. King's monsters are found not on planets light years away or in other exotic or foreign locations. Instead, they inhabit the groundfloors of American factories, high schools, and rectories. Some of his creatures prowl the dark recesses of woods and swamps, but his most frightening creations can be found in neighborhood communities occupying positions of power and authority or in Washington controlling the fate of the nation. Like *Rosemary's Baby* and *The Exorcist*, King's world is an easily recognizable one, and when terror is unleashed in that world it becomes all the more terrifying because we comprehend its immediate relevance to our daily lives.

2

It is his awareness of the pervasiveness of evil—indeed, that it exists in ourselves, our social and political institutions, in short, in everything human—that links King to the literary tradition of American gothicism. In his essay "King and the Literary Tradition of Horror and the Supernatural," Ben Indick argues that King "has absorbed and utilized those qualities which characterize the different types of stories in the horror genre. In his own distinctive style are mirrored the major traditions he has inherited" (175). While Indick broadly outlines those gothic elements which have influenced King (e.g. the ghost story, vampire tale, etc.), he pays scant attention to the American romance tradition of the nineteenth century. Although he briefly includes mention of Poe in his analysis, Indick does not provide any thorough investigation linking King to Poe and other American writers from the nineteenth century. In fact, King owes as much to this earlier generation of writers—particularly Hawthorne and Twain—as he does to any German vampire legend or to his literary contemporaries, Blatty and Levin. The connection between King and the nineteenth century requires a critical forum for several reasons. The most important is by way of establishing King's place in the mainstream tradition of American literature. At the same time this relationship can also provide an appropriate context for discussing the origins of King's moralist vision.

The most obvious similarity that King shares with these nineteenth-century writers is his reliance on gothic settings and atmospheric techniques. Poe's haunted houses, Hawthorne's symbolic forests, and Melville's assorted workplace dungeons each bring to mind respectively *The Shining*, *Pet Sematary*, and "Graveyard Shift."

In Poe's tales of fantasy and terror, confined atmospheric environments are representative of the narrator's or main character's circumscribed state of mind. Thus, Prince Prospero's proud egotism in "The Masque of the Red Death" is illustrated by his seven-chambered castle sealed off from the world by metal doors and thick stained glass windows; the narrator's mental anguish in "The Pit and the Pendulum" is reflected in his dark, gradually narrowing prison cell; and similarly, the Usher mansion is emblematic of Roderick Usher's mental status: both its interior apartments and external facade exist in a state of chaos and disintegration.

The jump from Poe to King is really more of a skip, as their protagonists often find themselves in similar claustrophobic circumstances. In Poe's fiction, as Frederick Frank points out in his essay "The Gothic Romance," "Place becomes personality, as every corner and dark recess exudes a remorseless aliveness and often a vile intelligence" (14). King likewise employs physical settings as a mirror to a character's psychological condition, and *The Shining*, *'Salem's Lot*, "Graveyard Shift," "Strawberry Spring," "The Boogeyman," and "The Raft" are his most instructive examples. His gothic landscapes are animated by a terrible potency that appears out of all proportion to the small and vulnerable humans who are held within its bondage. Like Poe's buildings, King's architecture is imbued with a life of its own, an unnatural biology that reflects the character and history of its former inhabitants.

Although *The Shining* contains several explicit allusions to "The Masque of the Red Death," the Overlook's real inspiration is the Usher house, replete with its legacy of sin and death as well as its ultimate destruction. And similar to Poe's descriptions of the decayed mansion's relationship to its owner, the interior of King's Overlook hotel—with its dark, twisting corridors and infamous history—reflects Jack Torrance's own psyche. At the end of *The Shining* Torrance could no more depart from the Overlook than Usher could abandon the crumbling mansion that becomes his tomb.

Hawthorne's woods are a place of spiritual mystery; in them, young Goodman Brown, Reuben Bourne, and minister Arthur Dimmesdale must confront their own darkest urges. In *Pet Sematary*, Hawthorne's historical sense of puritanical gloom associated with the forest is mirrored in King's ancient Micmac Indian burial ground. Dr. Louis Creed, like so many of Hawthorne's youthful idealists, discovers in the Maine woods that evil is no mere abstraction capable of being manipulated or ignored. Instead, he finds his own confrontation with evil to be overwhelming, and like Hawthorne's Ethan Brand and Goodman Brown, he surrenders to its vision of chaos and corruption.

Melville's fiction, whether set on the sea or in the urban office, describes the quiet nightmare of a capitalist economic structure devoid of humanitarian principles. The workplace as structure devoid of humanitarian principles. The workplace as torture chamber is one of Melville's most frequent themes, and it is a vision that informs fiction as diverse as "Bartleby the Scrivner," *Benito Cereno*, and *Moby Dick*. The crew on board Ahab's *Pequod*, for example, is cajoled into blood oaths that force them to relinquish their humanity, becoming mere extensions of their mad employer's quest for personal revenge against Moby Dick. King's descriptions of work experience in contemporary America bear close similarities to Melville's: in "Graveyard Shift," "Trucks," and "The Mangler," his characters are forced to perform labor under similar dehumanizing conditions. For both Melville and King, gothic settings and apparatus are often evoked as vehicles for underscoring a sterile and rotting economic system.

Melville's urban and sea scapes and Poe's claustrophobic interiors make their regional influences difficult to pinpoint. Their use of gothic settings, while always specific and important to theme, could conceivably take place anywhere in the world; in Melville's sea novels and Poe's *Narrative of Arthur Gordon Pym*, for example, the macrocosmic backdrop of the ocean, because of its sheer enormity, floats the reader in a sort of salt water vacuum. Hawthorne, on the other hand, was at his best as a regionalist author. His sense of Massachusetts—as a repository for historical events as well as a physical entity—is intrinsic to his most important fiction. Hawthorne's New England forests and puritan ancestry function as living beings in his work; they are always subject to his closest scrutiny, and often exert a profound influence over the lives of his protagonists.

At the Conference for the Fantastic in Arts, held in 1984 at Boca Raton, Florida, I asked Stephen King, who delivered the conference's main address, what effect living in Maine had produced on his writing. He replied that "there's a Maine very few outsiders ever get to know. It's a place of rich Indian lore, rocky soil that makes it difficult to grow things, and incredible levels of poverty. Once you get out from behind the coastal resorts, the real Maine begins." King's Maine is a place of terrifying loneliness where nature seems antagonistic to human habitation and where men and women often feel the same degree of estrangement from one another as they do toward the supernatural creatures who threaten their lives. Burton Haden, perhaps the most persuasive critic on the regional influence on King, argues in "Beyond the Kittery Bridge: Stephen King's Maine," that in the writer's "myth of Maine" characters are confronted "with an overwhelming, terrifying challenge, and they won't survive it unless they can find within themselves some kind of courage that they didn't know they had" (59).

King is a regionalist in much the same way that Hawthorne was; each sensed that the real meanings behind the history and physical textures of a particular place could be fathomed only after great study—and what better laboratory than one's own ancestral past and regional legacy? Thus, *The Scarlet Letter* or "Young Goodman Brown" can no more be separated from their distinct puritan Massachusetts backgrounds than King's 'Salem's Lot or *Pet Sematary* can be extricated from contemporary Maine.

King captures the native speech patterns, the local raw materials of a cold climate, and the specificity of place that set his readers firmly in a rural Maine world. His north country is a region of a particular people, language, and customs, all set apart by an awareness of their differences from cities even as near as Boston. King returns over and over to descriptions of his native state, and he does so for some of the same purposes Hawthorne used in writing about Massachusetts: each author understands that the universal themes of great literature—human sin, fear, and endurance—can only be rendered truthfully within settings and by personalities an artist has come to know on a first-hand basis. Much as Hawthorne relied on puritan New England as a setting to describe the foibles and sins that are the inheritance of humankind, King views Maine as a deliberate backdrop for his own allegories, enabling him to utilize specific elements from that culture in his portrayal of the moral conflicts common to us all.

3

In his book *The American Novel and Its Tradition*, Richard Chase defines the most important aspects of the romance tradition:

> Astonishing events may occur, and these are likely to have a symbolic or ideological, rather than a realistic, plausibility. Being less committed to the immediate rendition of reality than a novel, the romance will more freely veer toward mythic, allegorical, and symbolistic forms. (13)

Chase makes these points with reference to the work of Hawthorne and Melville, but it is immediately apparent, even from what has been said only so far in this opening chapter, that the description also applies just as well to King. Indeed, as we shall see, the use of the horror story as sociopolitical allegory is one of King's major contributions to the genre. Like King, the nineteenth century possessed a similar interest in portraying the discovery of self through metaphors of motion, the journey quest, and the conflict between ideologically opposing forces. "William Wilson," *The Narrative of Arthur Gordon Pym*, "Young Goodman Brown," "Ethan Brand," "My Kinsman Major Molineux" *The Marble Faun*, *Moby Dick*, and *The Adventures of Huckleberry Finn* represent a blend of the literal with the symbolic, realism with allegory, and thus maintain certain similarities to King's canon.

The strength of King's stories is probably not to be found, however, in Melville's philosophical contemplations, nor in Poe and Hawthorne's speculations regarding the relationship between art and life. But the tentative and often precarious moral search for selfhood that characterizes the nineteenth-century romance tradition is likewise present in King. King's world-view is based on the complexity of modern life, and his protagonists begin the voyage toward moral wholeness only after experiencing the most disturbing encounters with evil. King relies on the journey motif in *The Stand*, *The Talisman*, *Pet Sematary*, and *Thinner* for the same reasons the nineteenth century did: the literal voyage—be it westward across contemporary America, downstream on the Mississippi River, or into the mysterious woods of a New England forest—becomes a metaphor for the journey into the self. This journey is fraught with danger along the way because King's young protagonists, like those of Twain and Hawthorne, learn that true moral development is gleaned only from a struggle with the actual, from confronting the dark legions of Morgan Sloat and Randall Flagg, rather than by avoiding them.

King writes fiction from the perspective of a fallen human world, and his characters commence their voyage to a moral comprehension of this world only at the very point where they become profoundly aware of the pervasive existence of evil. In Poe, Melville, Hawthorne and Twain, no individual is immune from the lure of evil—indeed, many of their characters succumb to its attractiveness and commit the most despicable acts of depravity. For example, neither Poe nor Melville satisfactorily explains why the narrators of "The Tell Tale Heart" and "The Black Cat" hate the old man and the cat, or why Captain Ahab feels the need to indulge his anger toward a white whale. However, there is strong suggestion that Ahab and Poe's narrators secretly hate what they see to be a reflection of themselves in the objects of their vengeance; for it is clear that in abandoning the most fundamental precepts of morality in order to accommodate the selfish urge to dominate and torment their fellow creatures, Ahab and Poe's narrators end up destroying themselves. Most of the other central protagonists from the canons of Poe, Hawthorne, and Melville are measured by similar ethical barometers: evil triumphs when the individual fails to exert control over his darkest impulses.

An analogous set of moral principles is at work in King's fiction as well. In *The Stand*, for example, those few remaining humans immune to the superflu are pulled between the two allegorical forces of good and evil, represented by Mother Abigail and Randall Flagg. Most of the characters who align themselves with Mother Abigail to establish a community in Colorado maintain their allegiance throughout, but *all* of these individuals— even the leaders of the group, Stu Redman and Nick Andros—are visited by Flagg, the latter appearing frequently in dreams of temptation, fear, and confusion. Only in actively confronting Flagg's influence do King's characters affirm the principle of goodness; Nadine Cross and Harold Lauder, on the other hand, succumb to Flagg's machinations because they lack the self-discipline necessary to exert a moral will.

4

The discovery of evil is the central theme that writers in the American romance tradition share with King. The writers in this tradition have created characters who are a complex blend of good and evil, often committing their greatest sins in refusing to recognize the evil in themselves. This encounter with evil is frequently overwhelming; it does not always lead to a higher state of being. In fact its discovery often takes a violent shape—destructive of the central character or of others around him. Jack Torrance, Louis Creed, and Harold Lauder, like Benito Cereno, young Goodman Brown, and Poe's psychotic narrators in "William Wilson," "The Black Cat" and "The Cask of Amontillado," are not spiritually transformed by their discovery of the darker side of reality, but succumb to its horror and retreat into cynical pessimism.

On the other hand, the nineteenth century also supplies us with the possibility for spiritual regeneration within its strict moral precepts. Twain's Huckleberry Finn, Melville's Ishmael, and Hawthorne's Hester Prynne, Dimmesdale, Donatello, and Miriam, learn that there can be a certain strength derived from a descent into the abyss. King's protagonists suffer intensely to uncover a similar truth. His young heroes and heroines—Charlie McGee, Danny Torrance, Jack Sawyer, Mark Petrie, and those adults who are either affiliated with them or embody many of their attributes—inspire us with their efforts against despair and toward moral advancement. In this sense there exists a level of salvation available to King's characters that binds them to the "survivors" in the canons of Melville, Hawthorne, and Twain: the knowledge that moral maturity is a possible consequence from contact with sin. Their protagonists learn that they have within themselves the capacity for making ethical choices, and that these decisions will either enhance or retard their adjustment to the reality of evil. Once this awareness is established, the opportunity for a new and more confident personality emerges. It is the portrayal of this evolution that finally links King's fiction to the moral vision available in the nineteenth-century romance tradition— the ability to uplift his audience with the promise that painful insights into the horrors of our world can propel us beyond egotism or cynicism and toward the theory and practice of redemptive sympathy. Perhaps King's protagonists are unable to articulate it quite so adroitly, but they are nonetheless in a position to understand and share in the same spirit of transformation that informs Miriam's personality at the conclusion of Hawthorne's *The Marble Faun*: "'. . . sin—which man chose instead of good— has been so beneficently handled by omniscience and omnipotence, that, whereas our dark enemy sought to destroy us by it, it has really become an instrument most effective in the education of intellect and souls'" (840).

Chronology

1947	September 21: Stephen Edwin King is born in Portland, Maine.
1949	Stephen's father, Donald King, abandons the family.
1961	Sells copies of his short story, based on a movie, at school.
1962	Graduates from grammar school.
1965	First published story, "I Was a Teenage Grave Robber," appears in *Comics Review*.
1966	Begins at University of Maine at Orono.
1967	Sells his first piece of writing, a short story appearing in *Startling Mystery Stories*.
1970	Graduates from Maine with a degree in English, a minor in speech, and a certification to teach.
1971	Marries Tabitha Spruce.
1971	Begins teaching English at Hampden Academy in Hermon, Maine.
1973	Doubleday accepts *Carrie*, King's first published novel.
1976	The film *Carrie* is released.
1976	*Salem's Lot* reaches the #1 spot on the *New York Times* bestseller list.

1977	*The Shining* is published and becomes King's first best-selling hardback.
1977	The first Bachman book, *Rage*, is published.
1978	*The Stand* is published.
1980	The movie *The Shining* is released.
1982	Publishes the first volume of the epic fantasy series *The Dark Tower*.
1982	Writes and acts in *Creepshow*.
1984	Collaborative book with Peter Straub, *The Talisman*, is published.
1985	Identity as Bachman is discovered.
1986	King-directed *Maximum Overdrive* is released.
1986	Film version of *Stand By Me* is released.
1987	Achieves sobriety.
1996	Wins the O. Henry Award for the short story "The Man in the Black Suit."
1996	Serial novel, *The Green Mile*, is published in six installments.
1996	"Twinner" book, *Desperation* by King and *The Regulators* by Bachman, is published.
1999	Severely injured when hit by a van while walking.
2000	Publishes short story "Riding the Bullet" and novel *The Plant*, only on the Web. Publishes *On Writing*.
2001	Publishes *Dreamcatcher* and *Black House*, a collaboration with Peter Straub.
2002	Publishes *Everything's Eventual: 14 Dark Tales*.

Works by Stephen King

BOOKS

Carrie, Doubleday, 1974

Salem's Lot, Doubleday, 1975

The Shining, Doubleday, 1977

Rage, as Bachman, Signet, 1977

The Stand, Doubleday, 1978

Night Shift, Doubleday, 1978

The Dead Zone, Viking, 1979

The Long Walk, as Bachman, Signet, 1979

Firestarter, Viking, 1980

Danse Macabre, Everest House, 1980

Cujo, Viking, 1981

Roadwork, as Bachman, Signet, 1981

The Dark Tower: The Gunslinger, Donald M. Grant, 1982

Creepshow, comic book of movie, Plume, 1982

Different Seasons, Viking 1982

The Running Man, Signet, 1982

Christine, Viking, 1983

Pet Sematary, Doubleday, 1983

The Plant, limited edition, 1983, 1984; serial novel, 2000–2001

The Talisman, Viking, 1984 (with Peter Straub)

Cycle of the Werewolf, limited edition, Land of Enchantment, 1984

Thinner, as Bachman, NAL Books, 1984

Skeleton Crew, Putnam, 1985

It, Viking, 1986

The Eyes of the Dragon, Viking 1987

Misery, Viking, 1987

The Dark Tower: The Drawing of Three, Grant, 1987

The Tommyknockers, Putnam, 1987

My Pretty Pony, Whitney Museum of American Art, 1988

The Dark Half, Viking, 1989

Dolan's Cadillac, Lord John Press, 1989

The Stand, The Complete and Uncut Edition, Doubleday, 1990

Four Past Midnight, Viking, 1990

The Waste Lands, Grant, 1991

Needful Things, Viking, 1991

Gerald's Game, Viking, 1992

Dolores Claiborne, Viking, 1992

Nightmares and Dreamscapes, Viking, 1993

Insomnia, Viking, 1994

Rose Madder, Viking, 1995

Desperation, Viking, 1996

The Green Mile, in six installments, Signet, 1996

The Regulators, as Bachman, Dutton, 1996

Wizard & Glass, Grant, 1997

Six Stories, Philtrum Press, 1997

Bag of Bones, Scribner, 1998

The Girl Who Loved Tom Gordon, Scribner, 1999

Hearts in Atlantis, Scribner, 1999

Storm of the Century, Pocket Books, 1999

On Writing, Scribner, 2000

Secret Windows, 2000 (expanded version of *On Writing*)

Dreamcatcher, Scribner, 2001

Black House, Random House, 2001 (with Peter Straub)

Everything's Eventual: Five Dark Tales, Scribner, 2002

From a Buick Eight, 2002

Sequel to *The Talisman*, date not set.

Cancer, date not set

The Dark Tower: The Crawling Shadow, date not set.

FILM

Carrie (1976)

The Shining (1980)

Creepshow (1982)

Cujo (1983)

The Dead Zone (1983)

Christine (1983)

Children of the Corn (1984)

Firestarter (1984)

Cat's Eye (1985)

Silver Bullet (1985)

Maximum Overdrive (1986)

Stand By Me (1986)

The Running Man (1987)

Pet Sematary (1989)

Graveyard Shift (1990)

Misery (1990)

Sleepwalkers (1992)

The Dark Half (1993)

Needful Things (1993)

Dolores Claiborne (1994)

The Shawshank Redemption (1994)

The Mangler (1995)

Thinner (1996)

The Night Flier (1997)

Quicksilver Highway (1997)

Apt Pupil (1998)

The Green Mile (1999)

The Girl Who Loved Tom Gordon (2001)

Stud City, independent film adaptation (in progress)

Hearts in Atlantis, 2001

The Sun Dog, IMax film (in progress)

The Mist (in progress)

Desperation, 2003

TELEVISION

Salem's Lot (1979)

This Is Horror (1989)

It (1990)

Sometimes They Come Back (1991)

Golden Years (1991)

The Stand (1994)

The Langoliers (1995)

Storm of the Century (1999)

Rose Red, miniseries (2002)

The Talisman, miniseries

Works about Stephen King

Anderson, Linda. "'OH DEAR JESUS IT IS FEMALE'": Monster as Mother/Mother as Monster in Stephen King's *IT.*" *Imagining the Worst: Stephen King and the Representation of Women*, ed. Kathleen Margaret Lang and Theresa Thompson. Westport: Greenwood Press, 1998, 111–125.

Ascher-Walsh, Rebecca. "Feast of Stephen." *Entertainment Weekly* (Feb. 19, 1993): 66.

Badley, Linda. *Writing Horror and the Body: The Fiction of Stephen King, Clive Barker and Anne Rice.* Westport: Greenwood Press, 1996.

Barrett, William P. "Sweet Charity." *Forbes* (Mar. 20, 2000): 180.

Beahm, George W. *The Stephen King Story: A Literary Profile.* Kansas City: Andrews & McMeel, 1991, revised and updated edition, 1992.

————. *Stephen King: America's Best-Loved Boogeyman.* Kansas City: Andrews & McMeel, 1998.

————, ed. *The Stephen King Companion.* Kansas City: Andrews & McMeel, 1987.

Blue, Tyson. *Observations from the Terminator: Thoughts on Stephen King and Other Modern Masters of Horror Fiction.* San Bernardino: Borgo Press, 1995.

Booker, Ellis. "Content Mgm't Net-Style." *InternetWeek* (Apr. 3, 2000): 82.

Campbell, Kim. "Can Online Book Publishing Stop the (Big) Presses?" *The Christian Science Monitor* (Mar. 15, 2000): 1.

Collings, Michael R. *The Many Facets of Stephen King*. San Bernardino: Borgo Press, 1985.

———. *Scaring Us to Death: The Impact of Stephen King on Popular Culture*, 2nd edition. San Bernardino: Borgo Press, 1995.

———. *Stephen King as Richard Bachman*. Mercer Island: Starmont House, 1985.

———. *The Works of Stephen King: An Annotated Bibliography and Guide*, ed. Boden Clarke. San Bernardino: Borgo Press, 1993.

Davis, Jonathan P. *Stephen King's America*. Bowling Green: Bowling Green State University Press, 1994.

Fink, Mitchell. "Horrormeister Stephen King." *People Weekly* (Jan. 19, 1998): 45.

Flamm, Matthew. "King's Ransom: The Horror Author Scares Up a New Deal." *Entertainment Weekly* (Nov. 21, 1997): 41.

Geier, Thom. "The Obsession of Stephen King." *U.S. News & World Report* (Sep. 23, 1996): 31.

Goldstein, Bill. "King of Horror." *Publishers Weekly*, 24 January 1991, 6–9.

Herron, Don. "Horror Springs in the Fiction of Stephen King," *Fear Itself: The Early Works of Stephen King*. Lancaster: Underwood-Miller, Inc. 1992. 57–82.

Hoppenstand, Gary, and Ray B. Browne, eds. *The Gothic World of Stephen King: Landscape of Nightmares*. Bowling Green: Bowling Green State University Press, 1987.

James, Darlene. Review of *Misery*, by Stephen King. *Maclean's* (July 1987): 51.

Kanter, Stefan. "The King of Horror; the Master of Pop Dread Writes On . . . and On . . . and On . . . and On." *Time* (Oct. 6, 1986): 74–80.

Kennedy, Dana. "Going for Cheap Thrillers." *Entertainment Weekly* (Feb. 23, 1996): 60–63.

Keyishian, Amy, and Marjorie Keyishian. *Stephen King*. Philadelphia: Chelsea House, 1995.

———. *Stephen King: Popular Culture Legends*. Philadelphia: Chelsea House, 1996.

King, Stephen. *Danse Macabre*. New York: Everest House, 1981.

King, Stephen. "On Becoming a Brand Name." *Fear Itself: The Early Works of Stephen King*. Lancaster: Underwood-Miller, 1992, pp. 15–42.

King, Stephen. *On Writing*. Scribner, 2000.

King, Tabitha. "Living with the Boogeyman." *Murderess Ink*, ed. Dilys Winn. New York: Workman, 1980.

Lang, Margaret and Theresa Thompson. *Imagining the Worst: Stephen King and the Representation of Women*. Westport: Greenwood Press, 1998.

Magistrale, Tony. *Stephen King: The Second Decade:* Danse Macabre *to* The Dark Half. New York: Twayne, 1992.

———, ed. *Landscape of Fear: Stephen King's American Gothic*. Bowling Green: Bowling Green State University Press, 1988.

———, ed. *The Dark Descent: Essays Defining Stephen King's Horrorscape*. Westport, CT: Greenwood Press, 1992.

———, ed. *A Casebook on* The Stand. Mercer Island, WA: Starmont House, 1992.

Miller, Chuck, and Tim Underwood. *Fear Itself: The Horror Fiction of Stephen King*. San Francisco: Underwood-Miller, 1982.

Pharr, Mary. "Partners in the *Danse*: Women in Stephen King's Fiction." *The Dark Descent: Essays Defining Stephen King's Horrorscope*, ed. Tony Magistrale. New York: Greenwood Press, 1992, pp. 19–32.

Reino, Joseph. *Stephen King: The First Decade,* Carrie *to* Pet Sematary. Boston: Twayne, 1988.

Russell, Sharon A. *Stephen King: A Critical Companion*. Westport: Greenwood Press, 1996.

Schweitzer, Darrell, ed. *Discovering Stephen King*. New York: Starmont House, 1985.

Saidman, Anne. *Stephen King, Master of Horror*. Minneapolis: Lerner Publications, 1992.

Spitz, Bob. "*Penthouse* Interview: Stephen King," *Penthouse* (April, 1982).

Underwood, Tim, and Chuck Miller. *Bare Bones: Conversations on Terror with Stephen King*. New York: McGraw-Hill, 1988.

———, eds. *Fear Itself: The Horror Fiction of Stephen King*. San Francisco: Underwood-Miller, 1982.

———, eds. *Kingdom of Fear: The World of Stephen King*. San Francisco: Underwood-Miller, 1986.

———, eds. *Feast of Fear: Conversations with Stephen King*. New York: Carroll & Graf, 1992.

———, eds. *Fear Itself: The Early Works of Stephen King*. Foreword by

Stephen King; introduction by Peter Straub; afterword by George A. Romero. San Francisco: Underwood-Miller, 1993.

Winter, Douglas E. *Stephen King: The Art of Darkness.* New York: New American Library, 1984; Signet, 1986.

WEBSITES

Horrorking.com's Stephen King Site
www.horrorking.com/

The Official Stephen King Web Presence
www.stephenking.com

Stephen King Page
www.malakoff.com/sking.htm

The Stephen King Net
www.stephen-king.net

Contributors

HAROLD BLOOM is Sterling Professor of the Humanities at Yale University and Henry W. and Albert A. Berg Professor of English at the New York University Graduate School. He is the author of over 20 books, including *Shelly's Mythmaking* (1959), *The Visionary Company* (1961), *Blake's Apocalypse* (1963), *Yeats* (1970), *A Map of Misreading* (1975), *Kabbalah and Criticism* (1975), *Agon: Toward a Theory of Revisionism* (1982), *The American Religion* (1992), *The Western Canon* (1994), and *Omens of Millennium: The Gnosis of Angels, Dreams, and Resurrection* (1996). *The Anxiety of Influence* (1973) sets forth Professor Bloom's provocative theory of the literary relationships between the great writers and their predecessors. His most recent books include *Shakespeare: The Invention of the Human*, a 1998 National Book Award finalist, and *How to Read and Why*, which was published in 2000. In 1999, Professor Bloom received the prestigious American Academy of Arts and Letters Gold Medal for Criticism.

CINDY DYSON has written several books for Chelsea House, and her work has been published in many national magazines. She's been a Stephen King fan since high school and particularly enjoyed writing this book.

A recent graduate of Pennsylvania State University with an MFA in Fiction, **AIMEE LABRIE** has published stories in journals such as *Beloit Fiction*, *Pleiades*, and *Scribner's Best of the Fiction Workshop* and book reviews in *CALYX* and *Willow Springs*. She works as a freelance writer and lecturer in English at Penn State and is revising her first novel.

MICHAEL R. COLLINGS has taught at the University of California and Pepperdine University and is a prolific writer in several genres. He has written numerous books on Stephen King and journal articles regarding the genres of fantasy and science fiction. He also has written several books of poetry and published short fiction and has contributed to numerous anthologies and periodicals.

Author of *Stephen King's America*, **JONATHAN P. DAVIS** is also a fiction writer with a work in progress. He has also written substantially on sports for *The Chicago Tribune*.

TONY MAGISTRALE earned a Ph.D. in 1979 at the University of Pittsburgh. Currently, he is an associate professor of English at the University of Vermont, Burlington. He has authored five books and served as an editor on two others.

Index